No Quarter *and* Th

These two plays were pr   t
the Hampstead Theatre   d
McWhinnie, who has co   is
volume. The volume also contains a short television scenario,
Invasion, which was presented by BBC Television in 1969,
directed by Donald McWhinnie in collaboration with the
author.

No Quarter is a play which exploits the traditional Chinese
theatrical device of showing events which take place in total
darkness. 'Its atmosphere is one of mounting terror; its
language that of common speech rearranged to produce effects
of comic incongruity and veiled threat; its themes human
solitude and the experience of waiting. . . . His dialogue has a
hallucinating power to dwell on commonplace objects until they
become strange and hostile.' *Irving Wardle*

The Interview shows eight strangers waiting for an interview –
gradually the interest of all focuses on one man. 'Soon he is
being bombarded with questions, orders, insults, political
feelers, flattery, and even a dissembled sexual approach. It
then becomes clear that their victim is the only genuine applicant. . . . The two plays by Barry Bermange establish him as
a writer for the theatre of considerable power.'

John Barber in the *Daily Telegraph*

In *Invasion* a room containing a group of diners is invaded
by the newsreel they are compelled to watch. 'A genuine break-
through in the acknowledged form of television drama.'

Stanley Reynolds in *The Guardian*

*The photograph on the front of the cover shows Felix Felton
in a scene from* NO QUARTER *at the Hampstead Theatre Club and
is reproduced by courtesy of Donald Cooper. The photograph on
the back of the cover is reproduced by courtesy of Christopher
Morris (Report: London).*

by the same author

NATHAN AND TABILETH *and* OLDENBERG

Barry Bermange

NO QUARTER
and
THE INTERVIEW

With an introduction
by Donald McWhinnie

METHUEN & CO LTD
11 NEW FETTER LANE · LONDON EC4

First published in Great Britain in 1969 by Methuen and Co. Ltd.

Printed in Great Britain by
COX & WYMAN LTD.,
LONDON, READING AND FAKENHAM

CONTENTS

INTRODUCTION

Bermange manipulates the elements of the dramatic illusion precisely and with complete control. *No Quarter* and *The Interview* are two of his cunning machines; you cannot change a word or a silence without doing damage. Such accuracy is rare in dramatic writing and has led critics to make a comparison with Beckett, though in subject and attitude there is no link; Bermange's theatre is his own creation and has its own mystery. What he does have in common with Beckett is his concern for words and for formal composition. The two texts in this volume are like musical scores; the notes on the page are exact and demand exact interpretation, the thematic development seems inevitable. It is this formal perfection, a counterpoint to the human, emotional factor, which gives the plays their special style. In *No Quarter* it is heightened by overt stylisation (of which the convention of 'darkness', the mimed violence, the absence of all but functional scenery are ingredients) and in *The Interview* by the rhythmic patterns of speech and silence and the ritualistic character of the action. Yet Bermange is not simply a stylist. The plays are deeply engaged with the human condition and deeply humane.

So perhaps it is not so strange to turn to *Invasion*, an invention which has a plot but no precisely formulated characters, a point of view but no written dialogue. Apparently it is a mere blue-print for a television programme. This is how it began; an idea which depended for dramatic impact on the conflict between two faces of reality: the coarse-grained, brutal, black-and-white world of the Vietnam newsreel and the colourfully refined, smaller world of the polite dinner party. The smart apartment was to be invaded by the actuality which

7

seems almost an illusion when we see it on the television screen; the room would be wrecked, the people destroyed, the colour drained away. The frivolous chatter would emphasise the horrors outside; they in turn would comment with bitter irony on the ephemeral enthusiasms exchanged over the smoked salmon. The author's concept was to treat a dilemma which we all face in a way which would hit us hard. Technically it was to be a calculated improvisation, containing elements which had been carefully selected and were to be controlled in performance, but leaving whole areas open to chance; a strict theme laid bare for spontaneous variation. Bermange was searching beyond words, now become inadequate; looking for chance correspondences and conflicts, for the accidents which make art exciting. Yet the blue-print had to be observed; this was not a free-for-all.

In practice what did this involve? The programme was recorded 'live' as a continuous whole, without stopping to amend errors or correct technical shortcomings; the machine started and ran on. The performers were free to talk and to behave however they liked, but with one proviso: each in turn had to be 'invaded' at a given point. The cameramen were free to take whatever shot appealed to them, but within a restricted area of operation, rather as an Outside Broadcast cameraman searches the sports stadium for interesting material. The vision mixer was free to select on the spur of the moment from shots offered by the four cameramen, but with the knowledge that exact effects were required at exactly timed moments. The technical effects – the destruction of the room, the draining of colour from the dinner party – had to be carefully rehearsed so that the combined creative contribution would not be interrupted and lose momentum. The simulated programme on the television screen in the apartment was specially compiled and edited to pinpoint the key moments of death and destruction. In fact there was a large element of pre-planning in order to leave the way clear for the exciting unpredictability of communal inventiveness.

Perhaps the atmosphere that was generated into the studio was more intense than that conveyed to the viewers; you could not expect them to share our sense of living dangerously, since it must have seemed to them that effects which we knew to be accidental were intended. Yet this strange blend of calculation and spontaneity almost certainly produced tensions which could not have existed in a more rigid production. Perhaps it is this quality of accidental inevitability which may explain why Bermange, a writer so concerned with words, should abandon words for a time. Naturally he could have written it all down instead of leaving it to chance; he could have scripted every shot and made sure that the finished result was exactly what he intended. Then, of course, it would not have been *Invasion* but something else. It was precisely the element of hazard which sparked off the programme and gave it its particular air of immediacy: a combination of free elements operating independently to serve the author's concept and with the author's whole-hearted encouragement. Bermange is constantly putting the raw materials of his art under the microscope, weighing and testing them, looking for new syntheses. *Invasion* was an important step in his evolution.

DONALD MCWHINNIE

No Quarter

A PLAY IN FOUR SCENES

NO QUARTER was written for the stage in the Spring of 1962. A sound radio version was broadcast on 14 November 1962 when with Beckett's WORDS AND MUSIC it formed part of the 40th Anniversary Celebrations of the BBC.

An amateur stage production, presented by The Questors Theatre Company, London, in 1964, was later re-staged at the Akademie der Künste, Berlin, in the West German Drama Festival *Modernes Theater auf Kleinen Bühnen.*

The first professional stage production was presented at the Hampstead Theatre Club on 9 June 1969, with the following cast:

LANDLORD	Denys Graham
FAT MAN	Felix Felton
QUIET MAN	Denys Hawthorne
MILITARY MAN	Douglas Storm

Directed by Donald McWhinnie

An hotel in which all the lights have fused.
An elevated platform centre stage.
A black bed with wing tables in the conformation of a requiem bier.
A candle in a holder on the U.L. table.
A chair.
The action takes place in darkness on a stage which, unless otherwise indicated, should be brilliantly lit throughout.
The surface of the platform may be mirrored to give a reflected image of the play.
Other extensions of the hotel, including the staircase, should be established by suggestion in the area surrounding the platform.

I THE STAIRCASE

When the curtain rises the stage is in darkness.
Pause.
Brilliant top-light on the platform.
Enter LANDLORD *quickly with lighted lamp.*
He turns and backs slowly towards the platform.
He stops at the D.L. corner and listens.
Enter FAT MAN *carrying three large suitcases.*
Enter QUIET MAN *behind him.*
They grope blindly towards the platform.
LANDLORD *edges slowly to the D.R. then U.R. corner*
where he stops.
FAT MAN *and* QUIET MAN *follow.*
LANDLORD *edges away.*
They continue round the platform as though in darkness.
FAT MAN *cries out irritably.*

FAT MAN   How much further are you taking us!
LANDLORD   Not far to go now, sir.
FAT MAN   We must be nearing the roof!
LANDLORD   The next landing will see us there.
FAT MAN   You said that nine landings ago.
LANDLORD   It's a big hotel, sir.
        One tends to lose one's bearings.
FAT MAN   One tends to get cold, too,
        at such an altitude.
LANDLORD   Yes, I'm sorry about that.
FAT MAN   I suppose your boilers aren't working.
LANDLORD   There's been a complication, sir.
        I'm expecting the man tomorrow.
FAT MAN   Of all the luck.
        The only hotel for miles

and nothing works in it.

No light. No heat. Nothing.

He cries out in pain.

LANDLORD *stops.*

LANDLORD Something wrong, sir?

FAT MAN My knee . . .

LANDLORD What about it?

FAT MAN I've knocked it.

LANDLORD Not on the banister.

FAT MAN Where else!

LANDLORD That's twice you've knocked your knee
on the banister.

FAT MAN I know.

You don't have to remind me.

He cries out again.

LANDLORD Stone a crow. You've done it again.

FAT MAN Don't just stand there. Do something!

LANDLORD What?

FAT MAN Turn on a light!

Oh my knee . . .

LANDLORD But I've already explained, sir.

FAT MAN My knee . . .

LANDLORD About the light I mean.

We've had a fuse blown.

That's the reason for the lamp.

He examines the lamp.

Fuses are very temperamental I might tell you.

They blow at the drop of a hat.

This one blew just before you came.

About a quarter of an hour before.

Pause.

Well, ten minutes.

FAT MAN My knee . . .

LANDLORD You see, Mr Barton, sir,

we're on one of them circuits where
if one light goes
they all go,
every last one of them. Well,
the one in the kitchen went.
Pause
Or was it the hall?
Pause.
No, no,
it was the kitchen one, the kitchen one.
Well, the kitchen one went
and the others went with it.

FAT MAN I don't care. Just get me to my room.

LANDLORD *looks up.*

Pause.

FAT MAN Our room.
Get us to our room
and be quick about it.

LANDLORD Follow me, sir.

He continues round the platform.

QUIET MAN *and* FAT MAN *follow.*

FAT MAN And don't hold that lamp so low.
We're almost in darkness down here.

LANDLORD *raises lamp.*

LANDLORD That better, sir?

FAT MAN *groans.*

FAT MAN These cases, these cases . . .

QUIET MAN May I carry one for you, Mr Barton?

FAT MAN What!

QUIET MAN One of your cases, Mr Barton.

FAT MAN Thank you. I'll manage.

QUIET MAN It would be no trouble, Mr Barton.

FAT MAN I'd rather you didn't.

QUIET MAN I would be

very very careful with it, Mr Barton.
I would take
very very special care
not to knock it or anything.

FAT MAN Please. It's all right.

QUIET MAN Very well, Mr Barton, you know best.
But it seems unfair
that a man of your age
should carry three big cases
up all these stairs
while a man of my age
carries none.
Apart from this
it would give me
very very great pleasure
to carry one. Or even two.
For you.
Now what do you say?
LANDLORD *calls.*

LANDLORD Well, sir!

FAT MAN What?

LANDLORD Mr Barton, sir!

FAT MAN What! What!

LANDLORD I asked if that was better, sir.

FAT MAN Better?

QUIET MAN He is referring to the lamp, Mr Barton.
Look.
He is holding it higher now.
FAT MAN *looks, then calls.*

FAT MAN Yes.
Yes, that's all right now!
They continue round the platform.

QUIET MAN Well, Mr Barton?

FAT MAN Well what?

QUIET MAN About the cases.

FAT MAN I've told you. No!

QUIET MAN I asked again
because I thought you might have
changed your mind.

FAT MAN Well I haven't.

QUIET MAN You would rather carry them yourself.

FAT MAN Yes.
I need no help.
I can manage
quite adequately
on my own.
They continue round the platform.
LANDLORD *stops downstage.*

LANDLORD Here we are, gents.
QUIET MAN *and* FAT MAN *join him.*
FAT MAN *sits on a suitcase.*

QUIET MAN Quite a climb, Mr Binks.

LANDLORD One gets used to it.

QUIET MAN Perhaps one day you will install a lift.

LANDLORD I've got a lift.
Pause.
It's out of order.
Pause.
Oh yes. I've got a lift.
You need a lift
in a place this size.
But it's out of order.
Trouble with the counterweight.
Yes.
The counterweight.
Been out of order for months.
Pause.
Counterweight trouble.

QUIET MAN You can't get it repaired?

LANDLORD You think I haven't tried?

I've tried all right.

God knows I've tried.

You think I can get it fixed?

QUIET MAN There must be someone. Somewhere.

LANDLORD I was recommended

to get in touch

with a man in Hornsey.

Know Hornsey do you?

QUIET MAN *says nothing*.

LANDLORD I must remember to get in touch with him.

FAT MAN *begins panting*.

Our friend here seems a bit puffed.

QUIET MAN The climb. It exhausted him.

LANDLORD You all right, sir?

FAT MAN *continues panting*.

LANDLORD You should have let him help you.

QUIET MAN *watches*.

LANDLORD When he asked

you should have let him.

Lugging that lot up here all by yourself.

You might have done yourself an injury.

FAT MAN *stops panting*.

FAT MAN Injury?

LANDLORD My word he does look queer, doesn't he?

QUIET MAN He'll be all right.

FAT MAN Did you say injury?

QUIET MAN A figure of speech, Mr Barton.

LANDLORD Flushed.

Flushed and drawn.

Don't you think

he looks

flushed and drawn?

QUIET MAN He'll be all right
after a good night's sleep.

LANDLORD You think so?

QUIET MAN Why not?

LANDLORD I'd hate there to be any
illness in the place.

QUIET MAN I can assure you Mr Binks
there is no danger of that.

FAT MAN Danger?

QUIET MAN A figure of speech, Mr Barton.

LANDLORD That's it.
A figure of speech.
Nothing to worry about.
He turns.
Come on.
Your room's down here.
He moves to the edge of the platform.
He stops, and faces the room.
QUIET MAN *and* FAT MAN *are left as though*
in darkness.

QUIET MAN Coming, Mr Barton?

FAT MAN Wait!
He rises from the suitcase.

QUIET MAN Yes?

FAT MAN What was he saying to you?

QUIET MAN Who?

FAT MAN Mr Binks.

QUIET MAN When?

FAT MAN Just now.

QUIET MAN What about?

FAT MAN About danger. And injury.

QUIET MAN He was just talking.

FAT MAN What about?

QUIET MAN Generally.

You know.
Generally.
FAT MAN *looks round uneasily.*
FAT MAN There's nothing going on,
is there?
QUIET MAN Going on?
FAT MAN You know what I mean.
Well is there?
QUIET MAN He's waiting for us.
He's down this corridor.
Our room's down here.
Coming?
He moves blindly towards the platform.
Come on.
It's perfectly safe.
Just pick up your cases.
And follow.
FAT MAN *picks up his cases.*
He moves blindly towards the platform.

2 THE CORRIDOR

QUIET MAN *and* FAT MAN *stop on either side of*
LANDLORD.
They face the room.

LANDLORD Here we are.
QUIET MAN Room Number 3281.
LANDLORD That's the one.
FAT MAN Open up!
QUIET MAN May we go in?
LANDLORD It's locked.

QUIET MAN What?

LANDLORD Safety precaution.

QUIET MAN But you've a key.

LANDLORD Somewhere.

He searches through trouser pocket.

FAT MAN Open up!

LANDLORD *continues search.*

FAT MAN What's keeping him?

QUIET MAN Ssh.

FAT MAN What's happening?

QUIET MAN The door of the room is locked.

FAT MAN Locked!

QUIET MAN Safety precaution.

FAT MAN He hasn't got a key?

QUIET MAN He's looking for it now.

LANDLORD *frowns.*

LANDLORD That's funny.

I could have sworn I had it on me.

It must be here somewhere.

Hold the lamp a tick someone.

QUIET MAN Here.

He takes the lamp.

LANDLORD Let me see now.

He continues the search.

FAT MAN *watches.*

QUIET MAN *gazes round.*

QUIET MAN How high up are we?

LANDLORD What?

QUIET MAN Are we very high?

Are we
in the clouds?

LANDLORD *continues the search.*
Silence.

FAT MAN *cries out impatiently.*

21

FAT MAN Well!

LANDLORD It must be here somewhere.

QUIET MAN Perhaps you've mislaid it.

LANDLORD Can't see how I could have.

QUIET MAN I have often mislaid keys.

LANDLORD Really?

FAT MAN Hurry! I'm cold!

LANDLORD Where is it?

FAT MAN What's the delay?

QUIET MAN The key. He's still looking for it.

FAT MAN I'm freezing!

QUIET MAN Patience.

He turns to the LANDLORD.
Which pocket
do you usually keep keys in?

LANDLORD This is the Sixteenth Floor.

QUIET MAN I suppose you've got a
special key pocket.

LANDLORD This one here.
This side one here.
Down here.

QUIET MAN And if it isn't in that one?

LANDLORD *looks up.*

LANDLORD What do you mean?

QUIET MAN Perhaps,
without realising,
you slipped it into another.

LANDLORD What?

QUIET MAN It's possible.

LANDLORD *and* QUIET MAN *face each other silently.*
LANDLORD *points to his trouser pocket.*

LANDLORD This is the key pocket. This!

QUIET MAN It isn't there, Mr Binks.

LANDLORD It must be.

He continues the search.

QUIET MAN Is there a hole in the pocket
by any chance?

LANDLORD *looks up.*

LANDLORD What are you insinuating?

QUIET MAN Merely
that if there is a hole in the pocket,
the key might have slipped through
to the lining.
Have you searched the lining?

LANDLORD *and* QUIET MAN *face each other silently.*

LANDLORD There isn't a hole.

Pause.

QUIET MAN That settles that then, doesn't it?

LANDLORD *continues the search.*

Silence.

FAT MAN *cries out impatiently.*

FAT MAN Mr Binks! I demand service!

QUIET MAN He's still looking.

FAT MAN This is an outrage!

QUIET MAN Relax, Mr Barton.

FAT MAN I am tired and I want to go to bed!

QUIET MAN You will. In good time.

FAT MAN I want to go now!

QUIET MAN We can't get in.

FAT MAN You mean he's lost the key?

QUIET MAN No.
But he has yet to find it.

FAT MAN What about the duplicate?

QUIET MAN *turns to* LANDLORD.

QUIET MAN He says what about the duplicate?

LANDLORD There isn't a duplicate.

QUIET MAN There isn't a duplicate.

FAT MAN There must be a duplicate.

QUIET MAN He says there must be a duplicate.

LANDLORD Well there isn't.

QUIET MAN There isn't.

FAT MAN *groans.*

FAT MAN Oh God. I'm so miserable.

QUIET MAN He says he's miserable.

LANDLORD I'm doing my best.

He continues the search.

QUIET MAN Look.

LANDLORD *looks up.*

QUIET MAN Why not try another pocket?

LANDLORD *points emphatically to the trouser pocket.*

LANDLORD This is the key pocket!

QUIET MAN It wouldn't hurt to try.

Just to make sure.

LANDLORD No!

Pause.

It wouldn't be in another pocket.

It couldn't be. I know.

I never put keys in them.

I put other things in them.

He looks up.

Wait a minute.

FAT MAN Has he found it?

QUIET MAN You've found it?

LANDLORD Give me the lamp.

QUIET MAN *gives lamp to* LANDLORD.

LANDLORD Yes.

I think I remember.

QUIET MAN *waits.*

FAT MAN *waits.*

LANDLORD It's all right.

Nothing to worry about.

I'll fetch it.
He turns to QUIET MAN.
You wait here.
He turns to FAT MAN.
With him.
He runs away quickly, twice round the platform and off.
QUIET MAN *and* FAT MAN *are left as though in darkness.*

FAT MAN *puts down cases.*

QUIET MAN *stands still.*
Silence.

FAT MAN Where has he gone?

QUIET MAN Down.

FAT MAN Why?

QUIET MAN For the key. The key to our room.

FAT MAN Will he be long?

QUIET MAN He may be a
very very short time.
He may be a
very very long time.
He may be back in a flash.
He may never be back.
FAT MAN *raises an arm and feels the air.*

FAT MAN This darkness . . .

QUIET MAN Does it worry you, Mr Barton?

FAT MAN No. Why should it?

QUIET MAN It might.

FAT MAN It doesn't.
He addresses an empty space.
Why do you ask?

QUIET MAN Many people are afraid of the dark.
He addresses an empty space.
Are you, Mr Barton?

FAT MAN Me?

Why should I be?

I've got nothing to be afraid of.

Pause.

Are you still there?

QUIET MAN I am here.

FAT MAN Be careful. Won't you?

QUIET MAN Of what?

FAT MAN The banisters.

Whatever you do

don't lean against the banisters.

They aren't safe.

In fact

if I were you

I wouldn't move at all.

No.

I wouldn't move at all

if I were you.

Silence.

QUIET MAN *and* FAT MAN *face front without moving.*

QUIET MAN We're very high up, aren't we?

FAT MAN We are.

QUIET MAN I thought we were.

We came up

thousands and thousands of stairs,

didn't we?

FAT MAN We did.

QUIET MAN I tried to count them.

I got to

nine hundred and seventy-seven.

Then you tripped.

I lost count when you tripped.

How many stairs

           do you think we climbed,
           Mr Barton?

FAT MAN Enough.
           Pause.
           What are you doing?

QUIET MAN Standing.
           Standing very very still.
           I like standing still.
           Silence.
           FAT MAN *cries out indignantly.*

FAT MAN He should have left the lamp!

QUIET MAN What for?

FAT MAN For us! For you and me!

QUIET MAN He needed it himself.

FAT MAN We are his guests!
           We have
           more right to it than he. Besides,
           our need for it is
           greater than his.

QUIET MAN Is it?

FAT MAN He knows his way around. Do we?

QUIET MAN Oh. Yes.
           Yes I think I know what you mean.
           FAT MAN *looks blindly for* QUIET MAN.

FAT MAN Have you been in this hotel before?

QUIET MAN Have you?

FAT MAN I'm asking you.

QUIET MAN It's such a big hotel.
           How high up did you say
           you thought we were?

FAT MAN I didn't say.

QUIET MAN I thought you did.
           Pause.
           What are you doing?

FAT MAN *and* QUIET MAN *look blindly towards*
each other.

FAT MAN What did you say your name was ?

QUIET MAN What ?

FAT MAN What ?
Silence.

QUIET MAN Why don't you stand still ?
It is nice to stand still.
FAT MAN *looks round blindly.*

FAT MAN This darkness . . .
Where does it end ?

QUIET MAN The darkness
makes us seem higher
than perhaps we are.
We do seem high, don't we ?
Pause.
Where are you now ?

FAT MAN Still here. I haven't moved.

QUIET MAN I thought I heard you moving.

FAT MAN You heard someone moving ?

QUIET MAN I thought it was you.
It must have been me.
Silence.
Pity about the lift, isn't it ?
FAT MAN *cries out incredulously.*

FAT MAN Lift !

QUIET MAN Mr Binks's lift.

FAT MAN He has a lift !

QUIET MAN It's out of order.
It's been out of order
for months now.

FAT MAN He might have said.

QUIET MAN He did say.

FAT MAN When ?

28

QUIET MAN You were out of breath.
That's when he said it.

FAT MAN Said what?

QUIET MAN That he has a lift.
That it's
been out of order
for months.

FAT MAN Some hotel I must say.

QUIET MAN He is
trying to get it fixed.
It isn't easy.
He has been recommended
to get in touch
with a man in Hornsey.

FAT MAN What man?

QUIET MAN A lift man I suppose.
He didn't say.
He just said
that he must remember
to get in touch with him.

FAT MAN What about?

QUIET MAN The lift.

FAT MAN What else did he say?
Silence.

QUIET MAN What?

FAT MAN What?

QUIET MAN What?

FAT MAN Did he say anything else?

QUIET MAN About what?

FAT MAN About anything.

QUIET MAN Anything?
FAT MAN *sighs.*

FAT MAN Oh, forget it.
Silence.

QUIET MAN Pity
it isn't working now.
He could have been
down and up
in no time.
As it is,
it will probably take him
quite some time
to make the journey.
Down.
And up.
Yes.
Quite some time I should say.
He smiles.
Unless . . .
Unless he runs.

FAT MAN *looks round blindly.*

QUIET MAN He may run.

FAT MAN It's outrageous!

QUIET MAN Running?

FAT MAN The way
this hotel is run.
I've
never seen anything like it.

QUIET MAN Seen
did you say?
That's funny.

FAT MAN No light. No lift. No boilers.
What does he take me for?

QUIET MAN And me.

FAT MAN I don't know about you.
He looks blindly for QUIET MAN.
What did you say your name was?

QUIET MAN *says nothing.*

FAT MAN   I don't know about you.
           But when I stay at an hotel
           I expect good service.
           I pay good money.
           And I expect good service.
QUIET MAN   That's reasonable.
           You pay good money.
           And you expect good service.
           Fair enough.
           But you
           can't hold it against him.
FAT MAN   I can.
           And I am.
           If he has the temerity
           to call this structure
           an hotel,
           he should run it as such.
QUIET MAN   You say he doesn't.
FAT MAN   I know he doesn't.
QUIET MAN   I think he's coming.
FAT MAN   *listens.*
           Silence.
QUIET MAN   No.
FAT MAN   You heard something?
QUIET MAN   It was nothing.
FAT MAN   *looks round blindly.*
QUIET MAN   *faces front without moving.*
FAT MAN   Where are you now?
QUIET MAN   Still here. You?
FAT MAN   Still here.
           Silence.
           He faces front.
           Did you notice
           that the rooms

31

have been numbered illogically?
Yes.
They jump from the
twenties to the sixties,
from the
thirties to the eighties,
from the
tens to the nineties,
from five
to one thousand and five!

QUIET MAN I didn't notice.

FAT MAN It's a fact.
No clocks either.
Not one clock anywhere.
Did you notice?

QUIET MAN I can't say I did.

FAT MAN It's a fact.
And something else.
He lowers his voice intimately.
On the seventh landing up
I saw
dead flowers in pots.

QUIET MAN Really?

FAT MAN I trod on a stair.
It crumbled.

QUIET MAN No.

FAT MAN All the way up
whole areas of banister
fell away.
Everywhere there is evidence
of decay.
You didn't notice?

QUIET MAN *says nothing.*

FAT MAN *cries out excitedly.*

FAT MAN Where are the other guests! Where!
Are there other guests!

QUIET MAN They are asleep.
In their rooms.

FAT MAN Yes, but are they?
Can we be sure?

QUIET MAN *says nothing.*

FAT MAN Where are you?

QUIET MAN *says nothing.*

FAT MAN *screams.*

FAT MAN Where!

QUIET MAN I am here, Mr Barton.

FAT MAN I thought you'd left me.

QUIET MAN Why would I do a thing like that?
I wouldn't do a thing like that.
Not to you, Mr Barton.
I like you.

FAT MAN It's not that I care.
I don't care.
Don't think I care.
Silence.
QUIET MAN *gazes round.*

QUIET MAN To think
that we are
so high up from the ground.
He smiles.
We must be in the clouds.
FAT MAN *gazes round blindly.*

FAT MAN Yes.
We must be.
Enter LANDLORD *quickly, with lighted lamp
and key.*
*He turns and backs slowly towards the
platform.*

C   33

He stops at the D.L. corner and listens.
QUIET MAN *and* FAT MAN *listen.*
Silence.
LANDLORD *returns round the platform at a slow steady trot.*

QUIET MAN That's him this time.

FAT MAN Hurry. Hurry.

QUIET MAN I can see the lamp.

FAT MAN Keep back from the banisters!

LANDLORD *continues round platform.*

QUIET MAN There he is.
Down there.
I can see him.
It's Mr Binks.
He's running up the stairs.
He has found the key.
He's coming up with it.

FAT MAN Hurry. Hurry.

QUIET MAN Up he comes. Up he comes.

FAT MAN Hurry. Hurry.

QUIET MAN Up he comes. Up he comes.

FAT MAN Hurry. Hurry.

QUIET MAN Up. Up. Up. Up. Up. Up. Up. Up.
A balanced rhythm is established between footsteps and voices.
It grows steadily louder, reaches a peak of great intensity, then stops abruptly as LANDLORD *comes to a standstill between* QUIET MAN *and* FAT MAN.
He faces front without moving.
Silence.
He raises the lamp.
Silence.
FAT MAN *picks up his cases.*

34

He faces front without moving.
QUIET MAN *faces front without moving.*
Silence.
LANDLORD, QUIET MAN *and* FAT MAN *turn and face the platform.*
Silence.
They step up into the room.

3 THE ROOM

QUIET MAN *and* FAT MAN *examine the room in silence.*
LANDLORD *watches them attentively.*

LANDLORD What do you think of it?
            QUIET MAN *smiles.*
QUIET MAN It is a charming little room.
LANDLORD It is rather nice, isn't it?
QUIET MAN Charming. Quite charming.
LANDLORD Yes it is. It is.
QUIET MAN *gazes round appreciatively.*
   FAT MAN *puts down cases.*
LANDLORD *watches.*
            Pause.
QUIET MAN It is a square room, isn't it?
LANDLORD A square room. That's it.
QUIET MAN Room Number 3281
            is a charming square.
LANDLORD Precisely. Absolutely.
QUIET MAN A charming square
            in the clouds.
LANDLORD Right up in the jolly old clouds.

And

soundproof into the bargain.

QUIET MAN An altogether delightful touch.

LANDLORD You think so?

QUIET MAN Indeed I do.

FAT MAN *listens.*

Pause.

LANDLORD Yes.

Yes you could

scream your head off in here.

And

nobody would hear you.

Shall I prove it?

QUIET MAN Please do.

FAT MAN No!

LANDLORD *and* QUIET MAN *look at* FAT MAN.

LANDLORD It would only take a sec.

QUIET MAN Go on, Mr Barton. Let him.

FAT MAN We've wasted enough time already.

LANDLORD It would only take a sec.

QUIET MAN What's a sec. Mr Barton?

LANDLORD You could spare a sec. Mr Barton.

QUIET MAN One sec. Mr Barton. Just one.

LANDLORD Just one. That's all.

FAT MAN *looks distrustfully at* LANDLORD *and*
QUIET MAN.

FAT MAN It won't take longer?

LANDLORD No longer.

Pause.

FAT MAN Very well.

QUIET MAN Good for you.

LANDLORD You come with me.

FAT MAN What!

LANDLORD Only for a sec.

FAT MAN What about me?

LANDLORD You stay here. In the room.

FAT MAN On my own?

LANDLORD And you come with me.

QUIET MAN Right.

> LANDLORD *and* QUIET MAN *move to the front of the platform.*
>
> FAT MAN *panics.*

FAT MAN Where are you taking him!

LANDLORD Outside the door.

> No further than the door.
>
> Come on.

FAT MAN You won't go away.

LANDLORD No further than the door, Mr Barton.

QUIET MAN Don't worry, Mr Barton.

> *Pause.*

LANDLORD Let's get started then.

FAT MAN What do I have to do?

LANDLORD Stay here. In the room.

> Wait for the signal.

FAT MAN Signal?

> LANDLORD *stamps his foot three times very slowly.*

LANDLORD Got it?

FAT MAN What do I do then?

> LANDLORD *smiles.*

LANDLORD Scream.

> *Pause.*
>
> LANDLORD *and* QUIET MAN *descend from the platform.*
>
> FAT MAN *cries out with terror.*

FAT MAN The lamp!

> LANDLORD *and* QUIET MAN *face front without moving.*
> *Silence.*
>
> FAT MAN *raises his hands.*
> *He turns slowly.*

He looks blindly round the room.
He reaches out.
He moves slowly towards the bed.
He stumbles against the bed.
He loses his balance, and cries.
He falls in slow motion on to the bed, face down.
He cries into the bed.
He sits up breathlessly.
He looks blindly round the room.
He reaches out.
He moves slowly from the bed.
He stumbles against his cases.
He loses his balance, and cries.
He falls in slow motion on to the floor, face down.
He cries into the floor.
LANDLORD *stamps his foot three times very slowly.*
FAT MAN *continues crying.*
LANDLORD *and* QUIET MAN *face front without moving.*
FAT MAN *looks up breathlessly.*
He panics.
He screams.
LANDLORD *and* QUIET MAN *face front without moving.*
Very long pause.
They turn and step back on to the platform.
They look down at FAT MAN.

LANDLORD You didn't scream.

FAT MAN I did!

QUIET MAN Incredible.
Silence.

FAT MAN *rises from floor.*
Silence.

LANDLORD Well then.
Once again.
I'm sorry I couldn't find

two singles for you but
as I explained
we are completely booked up.
Yes.
Booked up completely.

QUIET MAN Think nothing of it, Mr Binks.
I'm sure that
Mr Barton and I
will be
very very comfortable in here.

LANDLORD I hope so, sir.
I hope so.
There's just one final thing.
QUIET MAN *and* FAT MAN *look at* LANDLORD.
The geography of the room.

QUIET MAN Oh. That.

LANDLORD It's a
simple enough layout really.
As layouts go.
This . . .
He moves to the chair.
Is the chair.

QUIET MAN *moves to chair.*

FAT MAN *moves to chair.*

LANDLORD, QUIET MAN *and* FAT MAN *look at the chair.*
Long silence.

LANDLORD This . . .
He moves to the bed.
Is the bed.

QUIET MAN *moves to bed.*

FAT MAN *moves to bed.*

LANDLORD, QUIET MAN *and* FAT MAN *look at the bed.*

39

FAT MAN *tests the bed with his hand.*
Long silence.

LANDLORD This . . .

He moves to the D.L. corner of the platform, and faces front.

Is the wardrobe.

QUIET MAN *moves to D.L. corner.*

FAT MAN *moves to D.L. corner.*

LANDLORD, QUIET MAN *and* FAT MAN *face front without moving.*

QUIET MAN It's like a little room.

LANDLORD There are racks in it.

Pause.

Drawers and racks.

Pause.

Plenty of racks.

Pause.

And coat-hangers. Plenty of those.

Pause.

As many coat-hangers as racks, really.

Pause.

And a thin wire rail. For ties.

Pause.

You know. Ties.

Pause.

For anything, really. But mainly for ties.

Pause.

It's a tie rack, see.

Pause.

A tie rack.

Silence.

QUIET MAN Everything seems to be here.

LANDLORD *moves U.L.*

LANDLORD That's the bathroom.

QUIET MAN *moves U.L.*

QUIET MAN Through here?

He steps on to a square extension.
He looks round with interest.

LANDLORD All right, sir?

QUIET MAN Everything seems to be here.

LANDLORD Except a lavatory, sir.
There's no lavatory.
There's a
communal lavatory
on the landing. The last door.
You go out of here.
Turn right.
Go straight down the corridor.
And it's
the last door. You'll see it.
It's marked.
It's marked Lavatory.
You'll see it.
Pause.

QUIET MAN This is the sink then?

LANDLORD *moves to front of platform, and looks up.*

LANDLORD And this is the main light switch.
But we've had a fuse blown.
So you can forget that.

QUIET MAN *steps back into room.*

FAT MAN *gazes round uneasily.*

LANDLORD *turns and faces the bed.*

LANDLORD That's a table there.
By the bed.

QUIET MAN *moves to the U.L. table.*

QUIET MAN This?

LANDLORD Yes.
That's the table by the bed.

A bed-table.

There are two of them.

You can put things on them.

Anything you like.

QUIET MAN *looks at the tables.*

LANDLORD You'll find the Regulations
on that wall there.

QUIET MAN *moves to L. edge of platform, and faces out.*
Pause.

LANDLORD Well then.

That's all I think.

Any questions?

QUIET MAN Where is North?

Silence.

He turns.

He looks searchingly round the room.

North. Where is North?

LANDLORD North?

QUIET MAN I'd like to know
which way is North.

Do you know?

LANDLORD *looks blankly at* QUIET MAN.

QUIET MAN South would do.

Silence.

LANDLORD That's the bathroom.

Through there.

Those are the Regulations.

Pause.

I'd better be going.

Things to do.

QUIET MAN *smiles.*

QUIET MAN Thank you for all you have done.

LANDLORD My pleasure, sir.

He moves to front of platform.

He stops.

QUIET MAN *watches.*

FAT MAN *watches.*

Pause.

LANDLORD Should you require anything in the night.

You never know. You might.

There's a bell.

A nightbell.

On the wall above the bed.

Pause.

I don't suppose you'll need it.

Pause.

There again.

You never know, though, do you?

He descends from the platform.

He runs off.

QUIET MAN *and* FAT MAN *are left as though in darkness.*

FAT MAN Where has he gone?

QUIET MAN Away.

FAT MAN Why?

QUIET MAN Things to do.

FAT MAN What things?

QUIET MAN Things generally. You know. General things.

FAT MAN He has taken the lamp!

QUIET MAN That's right.

FAT MAN *raises an arm and feels the air.*

FAT MAN This darkness . . .

QUIET MAN Shall I strike a match?

FAT MAN *turns away slowly.*

QUIET MAN I'll strike a match.

He takes out a box of matches.

He lights a match.

FAT MAN *looks resentfully round the room.*

43

QUIET MAN There. Is that better?

FAT MAN This hovel! This pigsty!

QUIET MAN I think it is a charming room.

FAT MAN What's the smell in here?

Silence.

QUIET MAN Ah!

The match goes out.

FAT MAN *raises his arm.*

FAT MAN Where are you?

QUIET MAN Here.

FAT MAN Where!

QUIET MAN Here.

The match went out.

It burnt my fingers.

I had to drop it.

FAT MAN Light another! Quickly!

QUIET MAN *lights match.*

FAT MAN *looks round with awe.*

QUIET MAN Something wrong, Mr Barton?

FAT MAN There's no window in here.

QUIET MAN Why so there isn't.

FAT MAN There must be a window in here.

QUIET MAN Doesn't seem to be.

FAT MAN There must be!

Silence.

QUIET MAN Ah!

The match goes out.

FAT MAN *raises his arm.*

FAT MAN Light!

QUIET MAN *lights match.*

Silence.

FAT MAN There isn't.

QUIET MAN Don't worry.

It will be all right.

FAT MAN It's the thought
of being trapped
in a
windowless room.

QUIET MAN Try not to think about it.

FAT MAN I can't help myself.

QUIET MAN Try.

FAT MAN It's no use.

QUIET MAN Then
we must try to take your mind off it,
mustn't we?
Which way is North do you think?
That way? That way? That way? That way?
Which way?
And Hornsey?
Which way is Hornsey do you think?
That way? That way? That way? That way?
Which way?
Feeling better now?

FAT MAN *groans.*

QUIET MAN Ah!
The match goes out.
FAT MAN *raises his arm.*

FAT MAN Light! Light!

QUIET MAN *lights match.*
FAT MAN *looks worriedly at the flame.*

FAT MAN It's burning down again.

QUIET MAN Why so it is.

FAT MAN Light another one.

QUIET MAN Would you like me to?

FAT MAN Please.

QUIET MAN Supposing
I were to say
that

45

  this was my last.

FAT MAN Is it?

QUIET MAN My question first, Mr Barton.

 FAT MAN I don't know.

QUIET MAN What?

 FAT MAN I don't know.

QUIET MAN What?

 FAT MAN I don't know! I don't know!

   QUIET MAN *licks his fingers and inverts the match.*

QUIET MAN What?

 FAT MAN The match!

   QUIET MAN *and* FAT MAN *look at the match.*
   The match goes out.

QUIET MAN It is out.

 FAT MAN Light another!

QUIET MAN Why?

 FAT MAN Please!

QUIET MAN Mr Barton.

   You must

   pull yourself together.

   Surely you don't expect me

   to stand here

   striking matches for you

   all through the night.

 FAT MAN One more.

QUIET MAN Then another. Then another.

 FAT MAN Just one.

QUIET MAN There aren't many left.

 FAT MAN How many are left?

   QUIET MAN *counts them carefully.*

QUIET MAN Three.

 FAT MAN Use one of them now.

QUIET MAN That would leave us with two.

 FAT MAN While it is burning

I will
jump into bed
and go to sleep.
Please!

QUIET MAN Supposing you woke up?

FAT MAN You could strike another.

QUIET MAN And if you woke again?

FAT MAN The last.

QUIET MAN And if you woke again?

Pause.

You do see what I'm getting at, Mr Barton.
To burn matches now
would be wasteful,
wanton and wasteful.
Better to save them.
Much much better to save them.
Just in case.

FAT MAN In case what?

QUIET MAN Just in case.

FAT MAN Give them to me.

QUIET MAN Why?

FAT MAN I want them!

He lunges blindly.
He falls across the bed.

QUIET MAN *drops matches.*

FAT MAN *cries.*

QUIET MAN *looks blindly at floor.*

FAT MAN My knee . . .

QUIET MAN Now you've done it.

FAT MAN Done what?

QUIET MAN Made me drop the matches.
All three of them.
That was a silly thing to do.

FAT MAN Where are they?

47

QUIET MAN On the floor. Somewhere.

FAT MAN We must find them. We must look for them.

QUIET MAN You look for them.

> FAT MAN *reaches out.*
>
> *He rises from the bed.*
>
> *He moves slowly towards the floor.*

FAT MAN Help me!

QUIET MAN Very well.

> *He moves slowly towards the floor.*
>
> QUIET MAN *and* FAT MAN *move blindly round the room, feeling the floor and the air.*
>
> *They pass each other.*
>
> FAT MAN *moves U.L.*
>
> QUIET MAN *moves D.R.*

FAT MAN Where are you?

QUIET MAN Over here.

FAT MAN Where?

QUIET MAN Here.

FAT MAN Which way?

QUIET MAN This way.

FAT MAN I can't see!

QUIET MAN Walk in the direction of my voice.

> FAT MAN *rises.*
>
> *He moves towards the square extension.*

FAT MAN I am walking.

QUIET MAN You are walking away from me.

FAT MAN Help me!

QUIET MAN I can't see you.

FAT MAN Reach out towards me!

QUIET MAN I don't know where you are.

FAT MAN Walk in the direction of my voice!

> QUIET MAN *rises.*
>
> *He moves towards the D.R. corner.*

QUIET MAN I am walking.

FAT MAN You are walking away from me!

QUIET MAN Help me.

FAT MAN How can I!

QUIET MAN Where are you?

FAT MAN Here! Here!

QUIET MAN You are over by the door.

FAT MAN Am I?

QUIET MAN Reach out and see.

FAT MAN *reaches out.*

QUIET MAN Are you?

FAT MAN I can feel the handle.

QUIET MAN Turn it. Open the door.

FAT MAN *moves blindly on to the extension.*
Silence.
He cries out helplessly.

FAT MAN I'm in the bathroom!

QUIET MAN *turns slowly.*

QUIET MAN Perhaps I am at the door.
He faces front and raises his arms.
He reaches out.
I am.

FAT MAN Open it! Open it!
Pause.

QUIET MAN It is open.

FAT MAN Where! Where!
He moves back into the room.
He moves blindly downstage.
He falls over his cases and cries.

QUIET MAN Wait.

FAT MAN *lies quietly.*

QUIET MAN Listen.
Silence.
Enter MILITARY MAN *slowly.*
He moves blindly towards the platform.

He stops at the D.L. corner and listens.
QUIET MAN *and* FAT MAN *listen.*
MILITARY MAN *moves blindly round the platform.*
He reaches the front and stops.
He faces out.

MILITARY MAN Anyone home?
QUIET MAN Who is that?

MILITARY MAN *turns to face the room.*
MILITARY MAN Excuse me. Is this Room Number 3281?
QUIET MAN It is.
MILITARY MAN Thank heavens for that.
Lost my bearings on the way up.
What with the fuse and everything.
Had visions of spending the night
on the stairs.
Pause.
May I come in?
QUIET MAN Please do.

MILITARY MAN *steps up into the room, then up on to*
the bed.
He addresses an empty space.
MILITARY MAN Suppose I ought to apologise
for barging in like this,
but it's not entirely my fault.
QUIET MAN Oh?
MILITARY MAN No.
I was sent here.
QUIET MAN By Mr Binks?
MILITARY MAN Short stocky fellow.
Five foot six I would say.
With a moustache.
He directed me here.
Binks did you say his name was?
QUIET MAN Mr Binks.

FAT MAN *listens.*

MILITARY MAN He said the room was occupied.
Asked if I minded sharing.
No, I said.
I don't mind sharing.
As long as the person I'm sharing with
doesn't mind.
It's only for one night.
Just the one.
I don't mind sharing just for a night.

QUIET MAN Have you a light on you?

MILITARY MAN Sorry friend. Don't smoke.
Pity about the fuse.

QUIET MAN I don't mind the dark.

MILITARY MAN Not so bad
if you know where you are.
Tricky in a strange hotel though.
Did Binks explain
why the fuse had blown?

QUIET MAN He may have done.
I can't remember.

MILITARY MAN That's the trouble
with this kind of circuit.
One light goes
they all go,
every last one of them.
That what he told you?

QUIET MAN *says nothing.*

FAT MAN *listens.*

MILITARY MAN Still.
We've got the candle.
Let's be thankful for that.

QUIET MAN The candle?

MILITARY MAN Didn't he tell you?

QUIET MAN What about?

MILITARY MAN About the candle.

QUIET MAN He said nothing about a candle.

MILITARY MAN Funny.

He looks blindly round the room.

Know anything

about the

layout in here?

QUIET MAN The geography of the room?

MILITARY MAN The layout.

Where everything is.

The general set-up here.

QUIET MAN *looks blindly round the room.*

QUIET MAN The room

is a charming square.

In the clouds.

MILITARY MAN What?

QUIET MAN *says nothing.*

FAT MAN *listens.*

MILITARY MAN Know where the bed is, friend?

QUIET MAN Facing the door.

MILITARY MAN Straight across, right?

QUIET MAN Right.

MILITARY MAN Right.

He moves.

QUIET MAN Mind the cases.

MILITARY MAN *pauses, leg in air.*

QUIET MAN There are some cases.

On the floor.

I don't know where exactly.

Three of them.

Somewhere.

Be very very careful.

MILITARY MAN I'll take it steady.

He steps down from the bed.
He moves blindly to the chair.
He turns.
He passes QUIET MAN.
He moves slowly across the room.
His foot touches FAT MAN *who shrinks away.*
He returns to the front of the platform.
He turns.
He moves blindly to the bed.
Here we are.

QUIET MAN Found it?

MILITARY MAN I've found the bed.
Which side is the table?

QUIET MAN You'll come to it.

MILITARY MAN *moves blindly to the U.L. table.*

MILITARY MAN I've got it.
His hand moves slowly to the candle-holder.
And I think
I've got
the candle.
His hand moves slowly to the candle.
Yes.
Panic over.
Do you have a match?

QUIET MAN I have three matches.

MILITARY MAN Could you light one and bring it over?

QUIET MAN I'm afraid I can't do that.

MILITARY MAN Oh?

QUIET MAN No. No I can't do that.

MILITARY MAN Why?

QUIET MAN Because I do not have three matches.

MILITARY MAN *waits.*

FAT MAN *listens.*

QUIET MAN I had three matches.

Pause.
But I do not have them now.
Pause.
I had them before.
Pause.
Then something happened.
Pause.
Now I no longer have them.

MILITARY MAN Where are they?

QUIET MAN My matches
are on the floor. Somewhere.
I don't know where.

MILITARY MAN Couldn't you look for them?

QUIET MAN I could.

MILITARY MAN Would you?

QUIET MAN Would you like me to?

MILITARY MAN Well.
Without matches no candle.
If you see what I mean.

QUIET MAN *says nothing.*

MILITARY MAN Go on.
Have another look for them.
Feel around.
See if you can find them.
Pause.

QUIET MAN Yes.
I'll feel around for them.

MILITARY MAN There's a good chap.

QUIET MAN *moves slowly to the floor.*
He crawls blindly across the room, feeling the floor.
He touches a match.
He stops.
Any luck?

QUIET MAN It may be a dead one.

MILITARY MAN Let's give it a try, shall we?

QUIET MAN All right.

MILITARY MAN Hand it over then.

QUIET MAN Don't you want me to give it a try?

MILITARY MAN If you like. I don't mind.

Pause.

QUIET MAN No.

No you try.

I would rather you tried.

MILITARY MAN Let's have it then.

QUIET MAN *looks round blindly.*

FAT MAN *listens.*

MILITARY MAN *waits.*

QUIET MAN Where are you?

MILITARY MAN By the bed-table.

QUIET MAN I can't see you.

MILITARY MAN Walk towards my voice.

QUIET MAN Yes. I'll walk towards your voice.

He rises.

He moves blindly to the bed.

He moves blindly to the U.L. table.

He reaches out.

He touches MILITARY MAN.

They recoil with a gasp, then laugh.

QUIET MAN *holds out the match.*

MILITARY MAN *reaches out blindly.*

Their hands pass.

They seek to find each other.

They touch, then laugh.

MILITARY MAN *takes the match.*

QUIET MAN *holds out the matchbox.*

MILITARY MAN *reaches out blindly.*

Their hands pass.

They seek to find each other.

They touch, then laugh.
MILITARY MAN *takes the matchbox.*

MILITARY MAN There.

Now.

He lights the match.

There we are.

QUIET MAN *and* MILITARY MAN *face each other silently.*

It was a live one.

QUIET MAN *looks at the flame.*

QUIET MAN The head of the match is red.

The flame is yellow.

MILITARY MAN That's it.

Now for the candle.

He picks up the candle-holder.

He lights the candle.

QUIET MAN Two yellow flames.

MILITARY MAN Two yellow flames.

Now we're nice and cosy,

aren't we?

QUIET MAN *studies the flames.*

QUIET MAN Two yellow flames.

MILITARY MAN Yes.

Two. Nice. Cosy. Yellow. Flames.

He blows out the match.

One. Nice. Cosy. Yellow . . .

He sees FAT MAN

He raises the candle-holder.

I'm sorry.

QUIET MAN Sorry?

MILITARY MAN I didn't realise

there were two of you.

QUIET MAN He is my friend.

His name is Mr Barton.

56

MILITARY MAN How do you do, Mr Barton.

     FAT MAN *says nothing.*

MILITARY MAN I suppose

I owe you an apology as well
for barging in like this,
but as I have already explained,
it is not entirely my fault.

     FAT MAN *says nothing.*

MILITARY MAN No doubt

you heard me mention
that I was directed here.

     FAT MAN *says nothing.*

MILITARY MAN By Mr Binks.

     FAT MAN *says nothing.*

  QUIET MAN *watches.*

Pause.

MILITARY MAN Strange, is it not,

that such an
out-of-the-way hotel as this
should be
fully-booked up,
especially at this time of year.
He smiles.
This will teach me
to book well in advance
the next time.
If there is a next time.
Personally,
I don't think
I will be passing this way again.
Silence.
He turns to QUIET MAN.
It's none of my business,
but why is he sitting on the floor ?

QUIET MAN Mr Barton,

I regret to say,

isn't feeling very well at the moment.

FAT MAN *explodes to life.*

FAT MAN Lies! Lies! Lies!

I'm as

sound as a bell

in wind and limb.

He rises.

QUIET MAN My mistake.

FAT MAN The only mistake

is my presence here in this room.

I've had just about enough.

He moves to the bed.

He reaches up to press the nightbell.

MILITARY MAN I wouldn't ring that bell if I were you.

FAT MAN *pauses.*

MILITARY MAN It doesn't work, Mr Barton.

FAT MAN *turns silently.*

MILITARY MAN Surely the Binks fellow told you that.

He must have done.

Surely he told you

the bell was out of order.

FAT MAN *says nothing.*

QUIET MAN *watches.*

MILITARY MAN What's the matter with the man?

Has he no sense of responsibility?

Silence.

QUIET MAN He is just a man.

Silence.

MILITARY MAN *surveys the room.*

MILITARY MAN My.

This is a cosy quarter.

Is there a bathroom?

QUIET MAN Through here.

MILITARY MAN Keep my place. I won't be long.

> *He walks on to the square extension.*
> *He stands quietly, facing out.*
> QUIET MAN *picks up matchsticks.*

QUIET MAN Pleasant man. Don't you agree?

FAT MAN I don't care.

QUIET MAN You are past caring.

FAT MAN I am.

QUIET MAN Nothing matters any more.

FAT MAN My comfort matters.

QUIET MAN That sounds selfish.

FAT MAN Can I help it if I'm a selfish man?
> Outside Forces make me selfish,
> the same way they make a man
> lustful, greedy, cruel.
> He is none of these things to begin with.
> He is made this way by
> Outside Forces.

QUIET MAN Outside Forces?

FAT MAN People.
> Like him in there.
> Like Mr Binks.

QUIET MAN Like me?

FAT MAN I don't know about you.
> Perhaps like me
> you are also a victim.

QUIET MAN I have never considered myself a victim.

FAT MAN Does it matter what you consider yourself?
> Other people make you what you are,
> Outside Forces.
> It is the Outside Forces
> that make you what you are.
> *He yawns.*

59

I am consumed with fatigue.
I think I'll go to bed.
He moves to the bed, loosening his tie.
He sits on the bed.
QUIET MAN *rises.*

QUIET MAN I suggest that
as you are the largest amongst us
you had better take
the centre of the bed
because by doing so
you will be in no danger
of falling out.
Silence.

FAT MAN What did you say?

QUIET MAN I said that
I suggest that
as you are the largest amongst us
you had better take
the centre of the bed
because by doing so
you will be in no danger
of falling out.
FAT MAN *turns slowly.*

FAT MAN Are you suggesting
that I share the bed
with you two?

QUIET MAN Well.
There is the floor, I suppose.

FAT MAN Now look here young man.
I've been driven
far enough tonight,
right to the extremity
of my wits.
One more push

and I will not be
responsible for the consequences.

QUIET MAN But Mr Barton.

FAT MAN Mr Barton nothing!

QUIET MAN But Mr Barton.

FAT MAN *looks up swiftly.*

QUIET MAN Don't for one moment think
I do not appreciate
the state of mind,
the terrible state of mind
you are in.
I do. I do. Believe me.
But there are
certain facts we must face.

FAT MAN There is but one fact.
I am tired.

QUIET MAN So am I.
So is he.
We all care.

FAT MAN I don't care
about you two.

QUIET MAN I do.
He does.
Face facts, Mr Barton.
There are
three tired men
and one bed.
There is,
there can be
but one solution.

FAT MAN That I have the bed.

QUIET MAN That we share the bed.

FAT MAN I refuse to share anything.

QUIET MAN It may be a squeeze. But we'll manage.

FAT MAN I refuse to share.

QUIET MAN It will hold us all.

FAT MAN I refuse!

MILITARY MAN *turns and steps back into the room.*

MILITARY MAN Somebody refusing something?

FAT MAN You keep out of this!

MILITARY MAN Sounds like a revolt.

FAT MAN Yes! I am revolting!

MILITARY MAN You don't look too bad to me.

FAT MAN How dare you!

QUIET MAN *puts out his hand.*

QUIET MAN Mr Barton.

FAT MAN Let go of me!

MILITARY MAN What's going on?

QUIET MAN The sleeping arrangements.

MILITARY MAN What about them?

QUIET MAN There's only one bed.

MILITARY MAN So?

QUIET MAN There are three of us.

MILITARY MAN Where's the complication?

QUIET MAN *says nothing.*

MILITARY MAN *looks at* FAT MAN.

Pause.

FAT MAN If you think
I am going to share
that tiny bed with you two
you had better think again. Why,
the idea is outrageous.
Obscene!

MILITARY MAN *puts out his hand.*

MILITARY MAN Come come, Mr Barton.

FAT MAN Take your filthy hand off me!

MILITARY MAN My dear sir.
It is the

hand of peace I offer.
Silence.

FAT MAN Of what?

MILITARY MAN Of peace. Friendship. Understanding.
I understand your feelings.
Silence.

FAT MAN You do?

MILITARY MAN Of course I do.
And you have
every right to protest against
sharing a bed
with two strange men.
What normal self-respecting Englishman
wouldn't?

FAT MAN You see my point then.

MILITARY MAN As clearly as you
sit before me.
Pause.
I might add that
it is utterly refreshing
to meet a man
with an outlook on life as
moral and as pure and as decent as yours,
Mr Barton.

FAT MAN Thank you. Thank you very much.
But how does this affect
the sleeping arrangements?

MILITARY MAN Enormously.

FAT MAN How, exactly?

MILITARY MAN *turns.*

MILITARY MAN Friend.

QUIET MAN *turns.*

QUIET MAN You called?

MILITARY MAN Friend,

63

                    would you object to
                    dossing down on the floor?
QUIET MAN No.
                    Why should I?
MILITARY MAN Problem solved!
        FAT MAN And you?
                    Where will you sleep?
MILITARY MAN On the floor.
        FAT MAN And the bed?
MILITARY MAN Yours.
                    Pause.
                    All yours.
                    Silence.
                    Well now.
                    We had better look to it, friend,
                    and get organised.
                    Good job it's
                    just for the one night, what?
                    QUIET MAN *and* MILITARY MAN *laugh.*
                    *They move to the front corners of the platform, and sit
                    on the floor, facing the bed.*
                    *They take off their shoes, crawl forward and place them
                    under the bed.*
                    They loosen their ties and collars.
                    They lie down at an angle, feet towards the bed.
                    FAT MAN *regards them quietly.*
                    Silence.
                    He looks round the room.
                    He sees his cases.
                    He rises from the bed.
                    He crosses to his cases and brings them to the bed.
                    He gets on to the bed.
                    He looks at the men on the floor.
                    Silence.

He lifts the cases on to the bed.
He piles them one by one on top of him.
He lies back.
Silence.

MILITARY MAN Quite a neat little pattern,
isn't it?
The way we are lying.
The general disposition of bodies.

QUIET MAN Mr Barton is on the bed.
We are on the floor
on either side of him.
It is a
very neat pattern indeed.

MILITARY MAN Much much better than
scattering ourselves
higgledy-piggledy
all round the room. Why,
supposing one of us
were to get up in the night?
It would be chaos in here,
absolute chaos.
People falling over one another.
Bruising themselves. Ha!
Pause.
No.
This way is much better.

QUIET MAN It is.
I prefer this pattern best.

MILITARY MAN Oh yes.
Silence.
He sits up suddenly.

QUIET MAN *sits up.*

MILITARY MAN You see,
you've got to have Order.

E   65

Know what I mean?
Order with a capital O.
Without Order,
everything goes to pieces.
And when I say everything
I mean Everything,
with a capital E.
You can apply that to anything.
Order there must be
in anything and everything.
Yes!
He looks round the room.
And we've got it
in this room tonight.
Oh yes.
Pause.
If we've got nothing else,
we've got that.

QUIET MAN We have Order.
Pause.
We have Order in the clouds.
MILITARY MAN *and* QUIET MAN *face each other silently.*
MILITARY MAN *turns away.*

MILITARY MAN All right up top,
Mr Barton?
FAT MAN *calls from behind his cases.*

FAT MAN Yes. I'm all right.
MILITARY MAN No complaints?
FAT MAN None. None whatever. Everything is fine.
MILITARY MAN Jolly dee.

MILITARY MAN *and* QUIET MAN *lie down.*
Silence.

QUIET MAN We are a triangle.
Pause.

66

A triangle of men.
Pause.
We are three bodies sleeping together.
Pause.
And alone.
Pause.
We are a neat little pattern.
Pause.
We are a Trinity.
Pause.
We are the neatest pattern of all.
Silence.

MILITARY MAN Are you comfortable,
friend?

QUIET MAN I am.

MILITARY MAN Then I suppose it's time
for lights out.

FAT MAN *lowers cases, sits up slowly.*

MILITARY MAN Mr Barton.

FAT MAN Yes?

MILITARY MAN Blow the candle out,
there's a good chap.

FAT MAN Must I?

MILITARY MAN We can't sleep with it on, can we?

FAT MAN Can't we?

MILITARY MAN Suit yourself, Mr Barton.
If you'd
rather let it burn for a bit,
it's all right by me.

FAT MAN If you don't mind.

MILITARY MAN I'm easy.
And I'm sure
our friend is.

QUIET MAN Yes.

            I'm easy.
            Pause.

MILITARY MAN Blow it out when you are ready.
            It's all right by us.

FAT MAN Thank you.

MILITARY MAN Don't thank us, Mr Barton.
            Thank the Outside Forces
            that made us tolerant men.
            Pause.

MILITARY MAN Goodnight.

QUIET MAN Goodnight, Mr Barton.

            MILITARY MAN *and* QUIET MAN *begin to fall asleep.*
            FAT MAN *looks at them anxiously.*

FAT MAN Before you go to sleep
            there is something
            I have to say.
            It is
            rather in the nature of an apology.

MILITARY MAN *breathes softly.*

QUIET MAN *breathes softly.*

FAT MAN No, no.
            It is not in the nature of an apology.
            It is an apology. Purely and simply.
            I . . . It's like this . . .
            That's to say . . .
            I mean . . . I mean . . .

MILITARY MAN *sleeps.*

QUIET MAN *sleeps.*

            FAT MAN *regards them weakly.*

FAT MAN Outside Forces.
            Pause.
            They are at it again.
            He looks upward.
            Silence.

SCENE THREE – THE ROOM

He lies back slowly, under his cases.
The top-light fades to darkness.
The candle flame goes out.
A rumbling sound begins.
It fills the stage.
It spreads into the auditorium.
It grows steadily louder, reaches a peak of great intensity,
rumbles into the distance, and fades.
Long pause.
The top-light flashes on.
White dust is falling on to the platform.
A black beam leans at an angle from the stage.
Another hangs suspended.
LANDLORD *stands on the bed, head-bowed, white with*
dust.
MILITARY MAN *and* QUIET MAN, *white with dust, lie*
on the floor.
The white dust continues falling.
Silence.
It stops.
Silence.
MILITARY MAN *and* QUIET MAN *sit up slowly.*
They look round blindly.

MILITARY MAN What was that!

QUIET MAN It was a crash.

MILITARY MAN What was it!

QUIET MAN I heard it.

MILITARY MAN What was it!

QUIET MAN *looks blindly at the floor.*

QUIET MAN It came from inside.

Pause.

MILITARY MAN Funny.

Silence.

QUIET MAN Mr Barton all right?

69

MILITARY MAN *looks blindly at bed.*

    LANDLORD *stands silently.*

    QUIET MAN *listens.*

MILITARY MAN Mr Barton?

                You all right?

                Silence.

                Mr Barton?

                Silence.

                Mr Barton!

                Mr Barton!

    QUIET MAN Shake him.

                Gently.

MILITARY MAN I can't see him.

    QUIET MAN I'll light the candle.

MILITARY MAN No.

                I'll reach up

                and feel.

                He moves blindly to the bed.

                He feels the bed.

    QUIET MAN *listens.*

    LANDLORD *stands silently.*

    QUIET MAN Well?

MILITARY MAN Funny.

    QUIET MAN What?

MILITARY MAN He isn't here.

    QUIET MAN He must be.

MILITARY MAN The bed is empty.

    QUIET MAN It can't be.

MILITARY MAN Feel for yourself.

                QUIET MAN *moves blindly to the bed.*

                He feels the bed.

    LANDLORD *stands silently.*

MILITARY MAN *listens.*

    QUIET MAN The bed is empty.

MILITARY MAN *turns away slowly*.

    QUIET MAN Where has Mr Barton gone?

MILITARY MAN Ssh.

    QUIET MAN What?

MILITARY MAN Over by the bathroom.

    QUIET MAN What?

MILITARY MAN Someone breathing.

              QUIET MAN *and* MILITARY MAN *listen*.

    QUIET MAN Is it him?

MILITARY MAN Mr Barton?

            Is that you?

            Silence.

    QUIET MAN Did he answer?

MILITARY MAN No.

    QUIET MAN Is he hurt?

            Mr Barton?

            Are you hurt?

MILITARY MAN Are you hurt?

            Silence.

    QUIET MAN Perhaps he's fainted.

            The crash

            may have frightened him.

MILITARY MAN We'd better get up

            and see.

            QUIET MAN *and* MILITARY MAN *rise*.

            Coming?

    QUIET MAN I'm

            right behind you.

            MILITARY MAN *moves blindly U.L.*

            QUIET MAN *moves blindly D.R.*

            MILITARY MAN *stops*.

            QUIET MAN *stops*.

MILITARY MAN Here we are.

    QUIET MAN Where are you?

MILITARY MAN Over here.

Where are you?

QUIET MAN Over here.

MILITARY MAN What are you doing there?

QUIET MAN Following you.

MILITARY MAN I am here.

QUIET MAN You can't be.

I was following.

MILITARY MAN You couldn't have been.

QUIET MAN I was following somebody.

MILITARY MAN You couldn't have been following me.

I am here.

QUIET MAN Who was I following?

Silence.

MILITARY MAN Are you coming?

QUIET MAN Coming.

Coming.

He moves blindly across the room.

MILITARY MAN *addresses an empty space.*

MILITARY MAN Now, Mr Barton.

What are you doing out of bed?

And why no answer when we called?

You had us worried.

QUIET MAN Is he saying anything?

MILITARY MAN Nothing.

QUIET MAN He must have fainted.

MILITARY MAN Impossible.

QUIET MAN Why?

MILITARY MAN He's standing up.

QUIET MAN *pauses.*

MILITARY MAN Better light the candle,

friend.

QUIET MAN *takes out his box of matches.*

He lights a match, and turns.

He moves to the U.L. table.
He lights the candle.
He picks up the candle-holder, and turns.
He sees the feet of LANDLORD *on the bed.*
He stops.
He raises the candle-holder.
LANDLORD *raises his head.*
QUIET MAN *and* MILITARY MAN *look silently at* LANDLORD.

MILITARY MAN Well. Well. Well.

QUIET MAN Mr Binks.

LANDLORD Hello, sir.

QUIET MAN Hello.

MILITARY MAN *walks round bend.*

QUIET MAN *steps on to bed.*

LANDLORD *stands silently.*

MILITARY MAN And what,
may we ask,
are you doing here?

LANDLORD There's been a complication, sir.

MILITARY MAN *steps on to bed.*

LANDLORD *turns away.*

QUIET MAN *watches.*

MILITARY MAN What kind of a complication?

LANDLORD A collapse, sir.

MILITARY MAN Whereabouts?

LANDLORD In the West Wing, sir.

MILITARY MAN The West Wing?

LANDLORD The West Wing.
Yes, sir.

MILITARY MAN Serious?

LANDLORD Very.

MILITARY MAN Casualties?

LANDLORD Not sure, sir.

MILITARY MAN Not sure!
    LANDLORD Not yet, sir.
             Most of the rooms
             were empty.
             Silence.
MILITARY MAN You told me
             the hotel
             was full.
    LANDLORD Apart from the West Wing
             it was.
             Silence.
MILITARY MAN There's something wrong . . .
             with the West Wing?
    LANDLORD It just
             worked out that way.
MILITARY MAN There's something wrong . . .
             with the West Wing?
    LANDLORD Foundation trouble.
MILITARY MAN What kind?
    LANDLORD General.
             General.
             Silence.
    QUIET MAN There was a crash.
    LANDLORD That's right, sir.
    QUIET MAN A loud echoing crash.
    LANDLORD Echoing.
             Yes.
MILITARY MAN The West Wing is down?
    LANDLORD Practically.
MILITARY MAN Some is left?
    LANDLORD Bits.
MILITARY MAN What bits?
    LANDLORD One room.
MILITARY MAN Yes?

74

LANDLORD One landing.

MILITARY MAN And under them?

LANDLORD Thin air.

MILITARY MAN And over them?

LANDLORD Stars.
Silence.

QUIET MAN And over them stars.
Silence.

MILITARY MAN Have you seen
Mr Barton?

LANDLORD I haven't.

MILITARY MAN Are you sure?

LANDLORD Positive.
Is he missing?

MILITARY MAN You know he is.
Don't blush.

LANDLORD Who's blushing?

MILITARY MAN You.

LANDLORD I'm hot.
I've been running about.
Yes.
I've been running about.

MILITARY MAN You have been
standing right here.
In this room.
You heard us calling
Mr Barton.

LANDLORD You're right.
Yes.
I remember now. I did.
I heard you calling him.
I distinctly
remember hearing.
MILITARY MAN, LANDLORD *and* QUIET MAN *stand*

75

silently on the bed.
Long pause.

MILITARY MAN What were you
doing in our room,
Mr Binks?

LANDLORD I came
to tell you.

MILITARY MAN Tell us?

LANDLORD To warn you.
To warn you.

MILITARY MAN Warn us?

LANDLORD About the
West Wing collapsing.

MILITARY MAN You were here
when it collapsed.

LANDLORD That's right.
I was here.

MILITARY MAN Then you were here
before it collapsed.

LANDLORD In a manner or speaking,
yes.

MILITARY MAN *screams.*

MILITARY MAN Yes or no, Mr Binks!

LANDLORD *screams.*

LANDLORD Yes! Yes!
Silence.

MILITARY MAN Ready to warn us
if it did collapse.

LANDLORD I knew it was going to collapse.

MILITARY MAN You knew?

LANDLORD I was expecting it.
I've been expecting it to collapse
for donkey's years.
I knew about the foundation trouble,

see?

MILITARY MAN So you let us go to bed.
Then returned.
When we were sleeping.

LANDLORD Something like that,
yes.

MILITARY MAN You stood by us.
Ready to give the alarm.

LANDLORD Yes.

MILITARY MAN You came into our room
for no other reason.

LANDLORD Other than to warn you,
no.

MILITARY MAN For no other reason?

LANDLORD None.

MILITARY MAN *screams.*

MILITARY MAN No other reason at all!

LANDLORD *screams.*

LANDLORD None! None at all!

Silence.

MILITARY MAN There's nothing going on,
is there?

LANDLORD Going on?

MILITARY MAN You know.
Going on.

LANDLORD I don't know what you mean.

MILITARY MAN Don't you?

LANDLORD I don't.
I don't.
He looks away.
MILITARY MAN, LANDLORD *and* QUIET MAN *stand
silently on the bed.*
Long pause.

MILITARY MAN We'll discuss this later.

He steps down from the bed.

LANDLORD Where are you going?

MILITARY MAN To the
remains of the West Wing.

LANDLORD *steps down.*

MILITARY MAN Out of my way.

LANDLORD No.

QUIET MAN *steps down.*

MILITARY MAN Coming, friend?

QUIET MAN I am with you.

LANDLORD No.

MILITARY MAN Men may be trapped. Wounded.
We must rescue them.

LANDLORD You can't.

MILITARY MAN It is our duty.

LANDLORD You don't know the way.

MILITARY MAN You will tell us.

LANDLORD Oh will I?

MILITARY MAN Oh yes.

He smiles across at LANDLORD.
You will tell us.
Pause.
I'm a tolerant man, Binks.
Pause.
But I draw the line at cowards.
He spins round on LANDLORD, *his arms scissoring
upwards, his hands flying open.*
He freezes in a violent posture.
LANDLORD *stiffens, as though struck.*
QUIET MAN *watches the two frozen men.*
Silence.
LANDLORD *squirms slowly.*
He screams with pain.

LANDLORD Let go!

MILITARY MAN Tell us.

LANDLORD You're choking me.

MILITARY MAN The way.

To the West Wing.

Pause.

LANDLORD *screams.*

LANDLORD You are there!

This is it!

Brief silence.

The rumbling sound returns.

It fills the stage.

The top-light flashes quickly on and off.

MILITARY MAN, LANDLORD *and* QUIET MAN *sway from side to side.*

The floor's going in!

QUIET MAN What?

The sound spreads into the auditorium.

It grows steadily louder.

It reaches a peak of great intensity.

MILITARY MAN Jump for it!

On to the landing!

MILITARY MAN, LANDLORD *and* QUIET MAN *turn and jump together off the platform.*

The top-light flashes off.

Blackout.

The sound rumbles into the distance.

It fades.

4 THE LANDING

A dark silence.
Spotlights on MILITARY MAN, LANDLORD *and* QUIET MAN.

79

They stand downstage, facing out.
They do not move.

MILITARY MAN That's that.

QUIET MAN Our room has gone.

MILITARY MAN That's right, friend.
Our room has gone.
We no longer
have a quarter.

QUIET MAN No quarter.

MILITARY MAN None.

QUIET MAN We are on the landing.

MILITARY MAN Marooned.
Utterly and completely.

QUIET MAN We are marooned
in the clouds.

MILITARY MAN Precisely.

MILITARY MAN, LANDLORD *and* QUIET MAN *stand silently.*
You've got us
into quite a fix.
Haven't you,
Mr Binks?

LANDLORD *says nothing.*

MILITARY MAN *shouts.*

MILITARY MAN Haven't you!

LANDLORD Yes.
I suppose I have.

MILITARY MAN My friend and I
are curious to know
precisely what you intend
to do about it.

LANDLORD Do?

MILITARY MAN Do.

LANDLORD What can I do?

MILITARY MAN That is for you to decide.
We are in your hands now.

LANDLORD I feel so helpless.
I didn't account for this.
Not this.

MILITARY MAN Then you had
better start accounting.
It has happened!
It is real!

LANDLORD I don't know what to suggest.
This landing may go next.

MILITARY MAN That's right.

LANDLORD We'll all go with it.

MILITARY MAN Unless you
think of something.

LANDLORD What!

MILITARY MAN That is for you to decide.
You are responsible
for getting us up here.
You are responsible
for getting us down.
Pause.
Well?

LANDLORD I don't know.
I just don't know.
Spotlight on FAT MAN *lying face down under the angled
beam.*
His clothes are torn.
He is cut, bleeding, and covered with dust.
He groans.
MILITARY MAN, LANDLORD *and* QUIET MAN *turn.*
They look blindly towards FAT MAN.

QUIET MAN I heard a sound.

MILITARY MAN So did I.

    QUIET MAN It was a moaning sound.

                It came from over there.

       FAT MAN *lies still.*

    QUIET MAN *looks blindly.*

MILITARY MAN Can you see what it is?

    LANDLORD If only we had the lamp!

MILITARY MAN Can you see something now?

    QUIET MAN I do believe I can.

MILITARY MAN What?

    LANDLORD What can he see?

MILITARY MAN Ssh.

    LANDLORD I don't like it.

MILITARY MAN Quiet!

    LANDLORD I'm scared.

MILITARY MAN Hold your tongue!

    LANDLORD That thing over there.

                What is it?

    QUIET MAN I think it is a man.

MILITARY MAN Who?

                Silence.

    QUIET MAN It's Mr Barton.

                He moves L. from light to darkness.

    LANDLORD Where's he going?

MILITARY MAN To rescue Mr Barton.

                LANDLORD *screams.*

    LANDLORD He mustn't!

                Stop him!

                Stop him!

                MILITARY MAN *scythes the air upwardly with his arm.*

                LANDLORD *spins quickly to the stage.*

                QUIET MAN *stops, and listens.*

                MILITARY MAN *calls.*

MILITARY MAN Carry on, friend.

Everything's under control.
He moves R. from light to darkness.
QUIET MAN *continues.*
LANDLORD *lies still.*
FAT MAN *lies still.*
Silence.
QUIET MAN *appears at side of* FAT MAN.

QUIET MAN Mr Barton.

FAT MAN *lies still.*
QUIET MAN *touches* FAT MAN.
FAT MAN *looks up, his face red with blood.*
He screams.

FAT MAN Keep back!

QUIET MAN I am your friend.

FAT MAN Don't touch me!
Go away!
Leave me!
There's nothing
in the cases!
MILITARY MAN *appears in his spotlight.*
He calls.

MILITARY MAN What's he saying?

QUIET MAN Nothing in your cases,
Mr Barton?
FAT MAN *cries.*

FAT MAN Nothing.
Nothing.
They are empty.
All three of them.
Now leave me.

MILITARY MAN What's he doing?
QUIET MAN *answers softly.*

QUIET MAN He is crying.
He looks at his hand.

His tears
are on my hand.

MILITARY MAN Get him over here.

QUIET MAN Up you come.

FAT MAN *rises.*

QUIET MAN *turns away.*

FAT MAN Where are you taking me?

QUIET MAN Don't worry.

Pause.

You'll be all right.

Pause.

We are only marooned.

He moves R. from light to darkness.

FAT MAN *looks up.*

FAT MAN Marooned?

He moves R. from light to darkness.

Wait for me.

Wait for me.

Wait for me.

QUIET MAN *appears in his spotlight.*

Spotlight on FAT MAN *close by.*

MILITARY MAN We meet again,
Mr Barton.

FAT MAN Who is that?

QUIET MAN The other man.

FAT MAN What other man?

QUIET MAN The other man in the room.
There were three of us.
Remember?

FAT MAN *cries.*

FAT MAN There were more!

QUIET MAN Only the three of us.

FAT MAN There were more!

He looks round blindly.

84

Who else is here?

QUIET MAN Mr Binks is here.

FAT MAN Where?

MILITARY MAN Lying down,
Mr Barton.
He isn't very well.

FAT MAN Who else is here?

QUIET MAN Just the four of us.

FAT MAN And the others?

MILITARY MAN What others?

FAT MAN There are others
I tell you!

MILITARY MAN Who?

FAT MAN Men.
He looks round blindly.
Two men.
Pause.
They beat me.

MILITARY MAN When?

FAT MAN In the night.
Pause.
You were sleeping.
Pause.
Am I dead?

MILITARY MAN Physically no.

FAT MAN Technically?
He faces front.
I don't want to be.
Much too much
to be done.
Too many mistakes
to rectify.
False moves to correct.
Too many apologies

85

to make.
He cries.
I don't want to be dead!

MILITARY MAN You were saying.
About the men.

FAT MAN They beat me.

MILITARY MAN When did they come?

FAT MAN When you were sleeping.

MILITARY MAN You saw them?

FAT MAN The candle was out.
He remembers.
Not to begin with.
Pause.
To begin with
it was almost out.
Pause.
The wick floating
in a pool of wax.
Pause.
A floating flame.
Pause.
I lay there.
Pause.
Waiting for the darkness.
Pause.
Then it came.
Pause.
When it came
I heard sounds
in the corridor.
Footsteps. Whispering. Laughter.
It sounded like
people coming.
Pause.

They reached the door.
Pause.
They stopped.
Pause.
I lay there.
Pause.
The door opened slowly.
Pause.
I called out to them,
who are you!
Pause.
They came towards me.
Pause.
And then I knew.

MILITARY MAN Knew what?

FAT MAN What they were after.

MILITARY MAN What were they after?

FAT MAN *screams.*

FAT MAN My cases!

QUIET MAN They were empty.

FAT MAN *cries.*

FAT MAN I told them.
They laughed.
They thought I was joking.
I protested.
They beat me!
I must have fainted.
Pause.
Then I came round.
Pause.
I was no longer in the room.

MILITARY MAN Where were you?

FAT MAN In the corridor.
He screams.

Bleeding like a pig in the dark!
He raises his hands.
My face . . .

MILITARY MAN And the men?

FAT MAN They had gone.
Silence.

QUIET MAN It must have been them
I followed round the room.

FAT MAN Who were they?
LANDLORD *stirs, and groans.*

MILITARY MAN Ask Mr Binks.

LANDLORD Where am I?

MILITARY MAN On the landing.

LANDLORD What happened?

MILITARY MAN You bumped into something.
LANDLORD *looks round blindly.*

LANDLORD Mr Barton's here.

FAT MAN Who were they?

LANDLORD Who?

FAT MAN The men.

LANDLORD What men?

FAT MAN The men who beat and robbed me.

LANDLORD Who what?

FAT MAN Who beat and robbed me.
He covers his face with his hands.
LANDLORD *turns.*

LANDLORD I don't know what he's talking about.

MILITARY MAN You do.

LANDLORD I don't.
What men?
What men?

MILITARY MAN You tell us.

LANDLORD I don't know.
MILITARY MAN *hooks the air upwards with his arms.*

LANDLORD *screams.*
MILITARY MAN *screams.*

MILITARY MAN Out with it!
Traitor!

LANDLORD Let go!

MILITARY MAN Who were they!

LANDLORD I don't know!

MILITARY MAN Who!

LANDLORD *screams.*

MILITARY MAN Who!

LANDLORD Mr Green and Mr Brown!

MILITARY MAN You sent them here!

LANDLORD I sent them!

MILITARY MAN Lies!
You brought them!
Personally!
He hooks the air downwards with his arms.
LANDLORD *sprawls across the stage.*
He cries.

LANDLORD I didn't want to!
They made me!
They made me!

MILITARY MAN Scum!
He jack-knives his arms together.
LANDLORD *stiffens with pain.*
Silence.

QUIET MAN The cases were empty.

MILITARY MAN So what?
It is a question
of loyalty. Allegiance!
We are his guests.
Right left and centre
he has let us down.
Now it is his turn

to be let down.

LANDLORD *listens.*

QUIET MAN What are you going to do with him?

MILITARY MAN Make a man of him.

QUIET MAN How?

MILITARY MAN By giving him a chance to die
not neglecting
but doing his duty.
He relaxes.
While you were
out there rescuing Mr Barton,
I made a
brief reconnaissance of the landing.
I learned there is
still one feature of the West Wing
intacto.

QUIET MAN Which feature is that?

MILITARY MAN The lift shaft.

LANDLORD *sits up slowly.*

LANDLORD No.
I won't go.

MILITARY MAN I repeat.
Now it is your turn
to be let down.

LANDLORD *rises guardedly.*

LANDLORD No.

MILITARY MAN The rope will hold you,
Mr Binks.
You will descend the shaft
and sound the alert.

LANDLORD It won't hold me.

MILITARY MAN Then you will die a hero.

LANDLORD You can't make me.

MILITARY MAN You have no desire to

redeem yourself?

LANDLORD I'm not going.

He looks round blindly.

He screams.

Keep back!

MILITARY MAN You are going down the shaft,

Mr Binks.

LANDLORD Keep back!

MILITARY MAN You are going down,

Mr Binks.

LANDLORD *backs slowly into the darkness.*

MILITARY MAN *follows blindly.*

LANDLORD *screams.*

LANDLORD No!

MILITARY MAN *says nothing.*

LANDLORD No!

MILITARY MAN *says nothing.*

LANDLORD No!

MILITARY MAN *says nothing.*

Silence.

Sound of a long falling scream.

It fills the auditorium.

Silence.

LANDLORD *runs into his spotlight.*

He looks round blindly.

LANDLORD He slipped.

Pause.

The gates were open.

Pause.

I've been

meaning to get them fixed for ages.

Could I find anyone

to fix them?

Pause.

He leaned over
to open them.
Was it my fault
they were open?
Pause.
Nothing was my fault.
Pause.
The boilers. The fuse.
The bell. The lift. The gates.
Outside Forces.
Know what I mean?
They were responsible.
Not me.
I'm not guilty of anything.
I'm all right.
And I'll redeem myself.
You wait and see if I don't.
He turns to face the darkness.

QUIET MAN Where are you going,
Mr Binks?

LANDLORD To look for the men.
Pause.
Mr Brown and Mr Green.
Pause.
They'll vouchsafe for my character.
Pause.
They'll vouchsafe for my character.
Silence.
He runs quickly into the darkness.
Spotlights on QUIET MAN *and* FAT MAN *only.*
They face front.
They do not move.
FAT MAN *lowers his hands from his face.*

FAT MAN Where are you?

QUIET MAN I am here.

FAT MAN And the others?

QUIET MAN They have all gone away.

FAT MAN Will they be back?

QUIET MAN They might be.
It's hard to say.
FAT MAN *raises his hands.*

FAT MAN My head . . .

QUIET MAN Is it hurting you?

FAT MAN When I move it.

QUIET MAN Try not to.
Stand still.
QUIET MAN *and* FAT MAN *stand still.*

FAT MAN Will we ever
get down from here?

QUIET MAN You mustn't worry
about that.

FAT MAN I want to know.
If we are
going to be stuck here forever,
there are
certain things I have to do.

QUIET MAN What things?

FAT MAN Mistakes to rectify.
False moves to correct.
Apologies to make.

QUIET MAN You have sinned?

FAT MAN Over. And over. And over.
Silence.

QUIET MAN You may
confess your sins to me. Not now.
Later.
When we are settled.
Meanwhile,

93

let us consider ourselves
in relation to the Universe as a whole.
Pause.
Determine
in which direction lies the North.
Pause.
Once we know this,
we will know where Hornsey lies.
Pause.
And ourselves.
Pause.
In relation to The World.
Pause.
We will do this standing still,
Mr Barton.
Pause.

FAT MAN Standing still.
Pause.
QUIET MAN Nothing terrible will happen to us.
Pause.
So long as we are standing . . . Still.
QUIET MAN *and* FAT MAN *stand still.*

Spotlights slowly fade.

A dark silence.

Curtain.

The Interview

A PLAY IN THREE SCENES

The Interview was first presented in a double-bill with *No Quarter* at the Hampstead Theatre Club on 9 June 1969.

The EIGHT MEN, in numerical order, were played by Felix Felton, Andrew Laurence, Donald Gee, Anthony Fox, Denys Graham, Denys Hawthorne, John Marquand, and Douglas Storm.

The SECRETARY was played by Hermione Boulton.

The play was directed by Donald McWhinnie.

A screen version of *The Interview* was televised by the BBC on 28 February 1968.

> *A Waiting Room bathed in a warm late afternoon light.*
> *A door U.L.*
> *A door U.R.*
> *Twelve chairs.*
> *A magazine table with ashtray.*
> *A painting (or relief) on a wall.*
>
> *The Men are called by their real names. In the text they are referred to by number.*
> *The floor of the room should be carpeted, silencing movement.*
> *The action unfolds slowly in a quiet and natural atmosphere.*
> *As it does so, the room gets steadily darker, filling with shadows.*

96

1 WAITING ROOM

When the audience enters, MAN ONE *and* MAN TWO *are already in position. (See below).*
Long pause.
MAN THREE *enters.*
Long pause.
MAN FOUR *enters.*
Long pause.
MAN FIVE *and* MAN SIX *enter.*
Long pause.
MAN SEVEN *enters.*
Long pause.
MAN EIGHT *enters.*
Long pause.
The house lights go out.
The men wait in silence:
MAN ONE *sitting, reading newspaper, eating.*
MAN TWO *standing, facing source of light.*
MAN THREE *sitting, reading book.*
MAN FOUR *standing, studying painting.*
MAN FIVE *sitting, watching the others.*
MAN SIX *sitting, watching* MAN FIVE.
MAN SEVEN *standing quietly.*
MAN EIGHT *standing, staring at floor.*
Long pause.
MAN ONE *turns page.*
Long pause.
MAN THREE *turns page.*
Long pause.
MAN FIVE *turns, sees* MAN SIX *watching him.*

They smile at one another.
Long pause.
U.L. door opens suddenly.
SECRETARY *enters.*
She smiles pleasantly.

SECRETARY Mr [*Full name of* MAN FOUR].
MAN FOUR *crosses to the chairs, collects coat and brief-case.*
MAN EIGHT *watches him.*
MAN FOUR *turns, sees* MAN EIGHT.
He smiles.
This way please.
MAN FOUR *goes through the U.L. door.*
SECRETARY *follows.*
The door closes.
Silence.
MAN EIGHT *stares at the door.*
He lights a cigarette, shakes out the match, looks round at the men.
He rises, moves to the ashtray, deposits match, moves to the painting, studies it quietly.
MAN SEVEN *and* MAN TWO *stand silently.*
MAN THREE *continues reading.*
MAN FIVE, *looking round, sees* MAN SIX *still watching him.*
They smile at each other.
MAN ONE *laughs suddenly.*
The men look at him.
He lowers the newspaper.
MAN ONE There's a job in here.
He looks round at the men.
Librarian.
Silence.

He shakes his head and continues reading.
The men wait.
He lowers the newspaper slowly.
The successful applicant will speak fluent Serbian.
Any offers ?
The men smile.

MAN EIGHT Where ?

    MAN ONE *consults the newspaper.*

MAN ONE Aldershot.

MAN FIVE *smiles.*

MAN ONE *continues reading and eating.*

MAN EIGHT Serbian ?

MAN ONE That's what it says.

MAN THREE Must be a Serbian library.

MAN EIGHT In Aldershot ?

MAN THREE Why not ?

MAN ONE I've never been there.

MAN THREE You should go.

    MAN ONE *looks up.*

MAN ONE Next Friday.

    Pause.

Weather permitting.
He winks at MAN EIGHT, *who smiles.*
He folds the newspaper, continues reading, then looks up slowly at MAN FIVE.
Coming ?
Pause.
We'll visit the Serbian Library.
MAN FIVE *smiles.*
MAN ONE *returns to the newspaper,* MAN EIGHT *to the painting.*
MAN FIVE *looks at* MAN SIX, *now facing away.*
MAN SIX *turns slowly towards him.*
MAN FIVE *turns away.*

MAN EIGHT *moves backwards from the painting, studying it thoughtfully.*

He reaches an empty chair, sits, smokes quietly.

He speaks suddenly.

MAN EIGHT I expect you've been there.

Silence.

He looks at MAN FIVE.

Have you?

MAN FIVE No.

MAN EIGHT Are you going?

MAN FIVE *says nothing.*

MAN EIGHT Don't you know?

MAN FIVE I may. One day.

MAN EIGHT Not planning to, right?

In the near future I mean.

MAN ONE He's coming with me.

He looks over the top of the newspaper.

Aren't you?

MAN FIVE *smiles.*

MAN EIGHT *smiles.*

MAN ONE *continues reading.*

Long pause.

MAN EIGHT Broadstairs.

Silence.

He leans forward, flicks ash from his cigarette into the ashtray, studies it thoughtfully.

That's a nice town.

Ever been there?

MAN THREE *looks up from book.*

MAN EIGHT *looks up at him.*

MAN THREE Me?

MAN EIGHT Have you?

MAN THREE No.

He returns to the book.

MAN EIGHT *looks at* MAN FIVE, *who shakes his head.*
He looks at MAN SIX, *facing away, then at* MAN ONE, *hidden by the newspaper.*
He looks at MAN SEVEN, *standing quietly, then at* MAN TWO, *facing the source of light.*

MAN EIGHT Nice town.

So is Whitstable.

Anyone been to Whitstable?
He looks round enquiringly.
Nobody been to Whitstable?
He continues looking round.
Bagshot?
Pause.
Peterborough?
Pause.
York?
Pause.
Been to York anyone?
That's a nice town.
He looks round.
No?
Pause.
Halifax?
Pause.
Devizes?
Pause.
Newton Abbot?

MAN THREE *looks up from book.*

MAN EIGHT *looks at him hopefully.*

MAN THREE *shakes his head.*

MAN EIGHT *looks at* MAN SIX, *still facing away.*

MAN THREE *returns to the book.*

MAN EIGHT *looks at* MAN FIVE.

MAN FIVE Once.

Silence.

He smiles.

I forget when exactly.

MAN EIGHT Fifty-five.

He nods slowly.

That's when I was there.

MAN SIX *listens.*

MAN EIGHT In the Autumn.

Pause.

We took a late vacation.

Pause.

Beautiful town.

Pause.

Lovely part of the world.

Pause.

You didn't like it?

MAN FIVE I only passed through it.

MAN THREE When?

MAN FIVE I forget.

MAN ONE *laughs suddenly.*

The men look at him.

He lowers the newspaper, gestures at something silly he has read, shakes his head, bites at some food, continues reading.

MAN EIGHT *looks at* MAN FIVE.

MAN FIVE *looks back at him quietly.*

MAN EIGHT I've an Uncle there.

I'm surprised you didn't like it.

MAN FIVE I hardly saw it.

It was on my way . . .

Pause.

I was going to Barnstaple.

MAN ONE From where?

MAN EIGHT Uncle Geoffrey.

MAN FIVE Salcombe.

MAN SIX *frowns.*

MAN THREE *nods slowly.*

MAN FIVE *looks at* MAN EIGHT, *who smiles.*

MAN EIGHT Dear old Uncle Geoffrey.

        Silence.

        MAN THREE *smiles.*

MAN THREE Swindon's a nice town.

        Anyone been to Swindon?

  MAN ONE *looks at him.*

MAN THREE You?

  MAN ONE No.

        He continues reading.

        MAN THREE *looks at* MAN EIGHT.

MAN EIGHT Once.

        Passed through on my way to Knaresborough.

        Anyone been there?

        All except MAN TWO *shake their head.*

        Long silence.

        MAN ONE *lowers the newspaper slowly.*

        The men look at him.

  MAN ONE I've been to Kettering.

        Silence.

        U.L. door opens suddenly.

        SECRETARY *enters.*

        She smiles pleasantly.

SECRETARY Mr [*Full name of* MAN SEVEN].

        MAN SEVEN *collects his things and goes through the U.L. door.*

        SECRETARY *follows.*

        The door closes.

        Silence.

        MAN EIGHT *rises.*

        He stubs out his cigarette in the ashtray, stands quietly

looking round, then moves to the centre of the room.
He looks at the U.L. door.
He looks round the room.
He returns to the magazine table and looks down at the magazines.
MAN FIVE *watches him.*
MAN EIGHT *looks slowly up at* MAN FIVE.
MAN FIVE *smiles.*
MAN EIGHT *nods, moves away from the magazine table, pauses uncertainly in the centre of the room, looks round at the men, then at the room.*
He moves to the U.R. door.
He opens it.
He looks round at the men.
He goes through the U.R. door.
The door closes.
Silence.
MAN THREE *closes and puts down the book, takes off and puts away his glasses, looks at and winds his wristwatch, rises, fingering his tie.*
He crosses the room towards the source of light.
He stops near MAN TWO, *who turns.*
They smile at each other.
MAN THREE *re-crosses the room, pauses at the magazine table, picks up a magazine, studies the cover while moving to a chair.*
He sits.
He continues studying the cover.
He speaks quietly.

MAN THREE Difficult isn't it?
Silence.
Don't you think so?

MAN FIVE *looks at him.*
MAN SIX *smiles.*

MAN THREE Sitting in a room with strangers?
Waiting for an interview for a job?

MAN SIX It's not too bad.
He smiles at MAN FIVE.
Is it?

MAN ONE He's used to it.
He looks at MAN FIVE.
Aren't you?
MAN FIVE *smiles*.

MAN FIVE It isn't my first interview.
If that's what you mean.

MAN THREE How many have you had?
MAN FIVE *begins to reply*.

MAN THREE Can't you remember?
MAN FIVE *smiles*.

MAN THREE Difficult isn't it?
Remembering things like that.
Details. Dates.
I think so.
He looks at MAN FIVE.
Were they all as difficult as this?
All those other interviews you've had?
I expect they were.
I expect you've had
quite a number of jobs in your time.
Pause.
Have you?

MAN ONE Nosy.
Laughter.
Movement.
Silence.

MAN THREE Can't remember how many I've had.
Pause.
Had quite a number though.

He looks round at the men.
Expect all of us have.
He looks at MAN FIVE.
I expect you have.
MAN FIVE *smiles.*
MAN THREE I expect you belong to that
floating population
they're always on about.
That's always on the move.
Here. There.
Up and down the country.
Job to job.
Place to place.
That you?
He smiles.
That your category?
MAN FIVE *begins to reply.*
MAN THREE Rather not say?
MAN FIVE *smiles.*
MAN THREE *turns away.*
MAN THREE It's hot in here.
Are you hot?
I'll open a window.
Shall I?
MAN FIVE As you wish.
MAN THREE *turns slowly to face* MAN FIVE.
MAN FIVE *looks back silently.*
MAN THREE What do you think of it?
Pause.
Do you like it?
Pause.
I suppose it's appealing.
If you like that sort of thing.
But is it Art?

He rises, and crosses the room.
He stops in front of the painting.
Is it Art?
He studies it quietly.
MAN FIVE *looks at painting.*
MAN THREE It's certainly restful.
MAN SIX *watches* MAN FIVE.
MAN TWO *stands quietly.*
MAN ONE *continues reading and eating.*
U.R. door opens suddenly.
Only MAN FIVE *turns.*
MAN EIGHT *enters, sees* MAN FIVE.
They face each other in silence.
MAN EIGHT *closes the door.*
He crosses to the U.L. door, pauses in front of it, then moves to the magazine table.
He turns, smiles at MAN SIX.
He picks up a magazine, and looks at it while moving to a chair.
He sits next to MAN FIVE.
He reads quietly.
Silence.
MAN ONE *begins reading aloud from the newspaper.*
MAN ONE 'Not a single discordant note . . .'
One by one the men turn their attention to him.
He continues reading aloud.
'. . . is there to be found in the picturesque little town, surrounding the picturesque little Church of Sainte-Foy, built, it is said, in the Eleventh Century, at the time when tourists were pilgrims on their blessed but footweary way to Saint James of Compostela.'
He eats some food.
The men wait.
He continues reading aloud.

'The play of light and shade in the Church interior, at its best in the Central Nave, emphasises, in no uncertain terms, the purity, the elegance, of the Romanesque style. The Last Judgement of the tympanum is, without doubt, one of the greatest, most uplifting examples of Romanesque Art. And the Treasure, of which the reliquary, in the form of a statuette of Sainte-Foy, is the major masterpiece, is, perhaps, unique in France, for from it one can follow the entire history of the Art of the Goldsmith from the Ninth to the Sixteenth Century.'

He eats some food.

The men wait.

He continues reading aloud.

'The town, it must be said, ranks with Chartres, Reims, Bourges, Saint-Benoit-sur-Loire, and Saint-Savin-sur Gartempe, in that in its midst can be found one of the richest, and most *evocatif*, of extant French religious buildings.'

Silence.

MAN THREE Which town?

MAN ONE Not telling you.

Laughter.

Movement.

Silence.

MAN EIGHT Travelled much have you?

MAN SIX *looks up.*

MAN EIGHT *looks at him.*

MAN SIX Me?

MAN EIGHT *nods.*

MAN SIX A little.

MAN EIGHT *looks at* MAN THREE, *who smiles.*

MAN THREE I've been to Macedonia.

A fine country.

A fine people.

MAN EIGHT *looks at* MAN TWO.

MAN TWO *turns, smiles, shakes head.*

Pause.

MAN ONE *looks up.*

MAN EIGHT *looks at him.*

MAN ONE I've been to Kettering.

MAN EIGHT *smiles.*

Silence.

He turns to MAN FIVE.

MAN EIGHT Have you travelled much?

MAN FIVE A little.

MAN SIX Like me.

MAN THREE Extensively?

MAN FIVE Here and there.

MAN THREE Where?

MAN EIGHT Specifically.

MAN FIVE *says nothing.*

MAN EIGHT Places. Countries.

Silence.

MAN FIVE In England mostly.

MAN SIX Never abroad?

MAN FIVE Once or twice.

MAN EIGHT South America?

MAN FIVE Europe mainly.

MAN THREE Germany?

MAN FIVE Mainly France.

MAN EIGHT Never Germany?

MAN FIVE Munich.

MAN THREE For long?

MAN FIVE A weekend.

MAN SIX Nowhere else?

MAN FIVE In Germany?

MAN EIGHT Yes.

MAN FIVE No.

MAN THREE You liked it?

MAN FIVE In Munich?

MAN THREE *nods.*

MAN FIVE It was all right.

MAN ONE Meaning he didn't.

MAN FIVE It was agreeable.

MAN SIX It broadens the mind to travel.

MAN FIVE I think so.

MAN SIX *nods.*

MAN THREE What about Germany?

MAN FIVE Munich was pleasant.

MAN ONE Meaning he hated it.

> *The men smile.*

MAN SIX You like the Germans?

MAN THREE (*to* MAN SIX) Do you?

MAN EIGHT (*to* MAN THREE) Do you?

MAN ONE (*to* MAN EIGHT) Do you?

MAN TWO (*to* MAN ONE) Do you?

> *The men look at* MAN TWO.
> *He turns away.*
> *The room is continuing to darken.*
> MAN THREE *speaks quietly.*

MAN THREE I don't mind them.

> *Pause.*

I can't forgive them.

> *Pause.*

I tolerate them.

> *Pause.*

MAN EIGHT *turns slowly to face* MAN FIVE.

MAN FIVE *looks back silently.*

MAN EIGHT Do you like Germans?

> I like your suit.
> *He touches the collar, gently.*

Who made it?
Your private tailor?
He runs his finger down the lapel.
It's awfully good material.
He runs his hand down the sleeve.
He looks up at MAN FIVE.
He speaks softly.
You like travelling then.
On the Continent.
Getting around.
You like that.

MAN FIVE Now and then.

MAN EIGHT In moderation.

MAN FIVE Yes.

MAN EIGHT Difficult for you is it?
Pause.
Getting away.
Pause.
Family ties?
Pause.
That sort of thing?
Pause.
Wife doesn't like it?
Pause.
Children cry for daddy.
Pause.
Not married?
Pause.
Divorced?
They face each other silently.
MAN ONE *takes his hand from the sleeve.*

MAN THREE I've got a
wife and two kids.

MAN EIGHT So have I.

MAN ONE Three kids.

MAN THREE No wife?

MAN ONE *stops eating.*

Laughter.

MAN ONE *opens a briefcase, and brings out a thermos flask.*

MAN EIGHT I've got two boys.

Billy and Sandy.

MAN THREE I've got a boy and a girl.

Nigel and Wendy.

MAN EIGHT Wendy!

MAN ONE Better than Sandy.

MAN EIGHT For a girl.

Yes. I agree.

All the men smile, except MAN FIVE.

MAN ONE *pours tea very slowly into the flask lid.*

MAN ONE I've got two girls.

He continues pouring.

And one boy.

He continues pouring.

Prunella.

He continues pouring.

Emma.

He continues pouring.

And Maximilian.

Silence.

He sips the tea.

MAN SIX *smiles.*

MAN EIGHT *looks at him.*

MAN SIX *shakes head.*

MAN EIGHT No family at all?

MAN SIX In Hornchurch.

A brother.

MAN EIGHT No-one else?

MAN SIX *shakes head.*

    MAN EIGHT *nods, then looks at* MAN FIVE.

    MAN THREE *crosses to a chair, sits, and looks at* MAN FIVE.

    MAN ONE *looks at* MAN FIVE.

    MAN SIX *looks at* MAN FIVE.

    MAN TWO *looks at* MAN FIVE.

    MAN FIVE *looks at the men.*

    Silence.

MAN FIVE I live with my sister.

    Pause.

    My wife is dead.

    Pause.

    Drowned.

    Pause.

    In a boating accident.

MAN EIGHT Recently?

MAN FIVE Eight months ago.

MAN EIGHT In Germany?

    Pause.

    You'd rather not talk about it.

    Pause.

    Forgive me.

    I'm being indelicate.

    He touches MAN FIVE *on the sleeve.*

    Forgive me.

MAN FIVE *says nothing.*

    MAN EIGHT *rises.*

    He moves to the magazine table, and looks down at the magazines.

    MAN FIVE *looks at the men.*

    All except MAN SIX *turn away.*

    He looks at MAN SIX.

    MAN SIX *nods.*

Pause.
U.L. door opens suddenly.
The men look up.
SECRETARY *enters.*
She smiles pleasantly.

SECRETARY Mr [*Full name of* MAN EIGHT].

MAN EIGHT *crosses to the chairs, collects his things, then moves to the U.L. door.*
He pauses in front of MAN FIVE.
They face each other silently.

This way please.

MAN EIGHT *goes through the U.L. door.*
SECRETARY *follows.*
The door closes.
Silence.
MAN ONE *finishes the tea, shakes some drops from the lid, screws it back on the flask, puts the flask away in the briefcase.*
MAN TWO *continues facing the source of light, the angle of which is changing, causing shadows to fill the room.*
MAN THREE *rises, and moves slowly to the centre of the room.*
He looks round at the men, then at the room.
He looks at the magazine table.
Silence.
He turns suddenly, moves towards the U.R. door, then stops, and looks at the floor.
He bends down, and picks something up.
He rises, studying it closely.
He holds it up.

MAN THREE A paper clip.

Silence.
He continues studying the paper clip while moving to the U.R. door.

He opens the door.
He goes out.
The door closes.
Silence.
MAN SIX *rises, and moves round the room.*
He stops in front of the painting.
He moves forward to read a panel on the frame.

MAN SIX It's got a title.

MAN ONE *looks up.*

MAN SIX *laughs.*

MAN FIVE *looks up.*

MAN SIX What a terrible title.

MAN ONE *folds the newspaper, and places it on a chair.*
He rises, crosses to the painting, and looks at the panel on the frame.
He laughs at it with MAN SIX.
MAN FIVE *smiles.*
MAN ONE *and* MAN SIX *slowly turn away from* MAN FIVE.
They discuss the painting silently, occasionally making gestures with their hands.
MAN FIVE *watches them.*
MAN TWO *remains silent, detached.*
The discussion continues, then stops.
MAN ONE *and* MAN SIX *turn, smiling.*
MAN ONE *looks at the painting, and shakes his head.*
MAN SIX *moves away, stops at the chairs, picks up the folded newspaper.*
He turns to MAN ONE, *raising the newspaper enquiringly.*
MAN ONE *looks at him, and nods.*
MAN SIX *opens the newspaper, and stands quietly reading.*
MAN ONE *brings out some cigarettes, takes one, pauses.*
He moves towards the source of light, and offers one to MAN TWO, *who declines with a smile.*

He moves back across the room, pauses, turns, offers one to MAN SIX, *who accepts.*

MAN SIX Thanks.

> MAN ONE *crosses to* MAN FIVE, *and offers him a cigarette.*
>
> MAN FIVE *shakes his head.*

MAN ONE Take one.

Do you good.

MAN FIVE I don't smoke.

MAN ONE Given up?

MAN FIVE I never have.

MAN ONE Frightened of catching it?

> *He smiles, and brings out some matches.*
>
> *He lights his cigarette.*
>
> MAN SIX *crosses to take a light from the match.*
>
> *The two men smile in the light of the flame.*
>
> MAN ONE *slowly shakes it out.*
>
> MAN SIX *moves away, and continues reading the news-paper.*
>
> MAN ONE *looks thoughtfully at* MAN FIVE.
>
> MAN FIVE *looks back at him quietly.*
>
> MAN ONE *moves away, and stops beside* MAN SIX.
>
> *He looks at* MAN FIVE.
>
> *Silence.*
>
> *The room is very much darker now.*
>
> *Only* MAN TWO *is clearly discernible, the others half in shadow.*
>
> MAN ONE *speaks quietly.*

MAN ONE Must have been a terrible shock.

> MAN SIX *looks up from the newspaper.*

A boating accident.

Pause.

Nine months ago.

MAN FIVE Eight.

MAN ONE As recently as that.
He returns to MAN FIVE.
That's why you're here.
To break with the past.
To start again.
New job. New faces.
Begin anew.
You saw the ad. in the paper, thought
'This is it.
I'll go along.
See what they're offering.
Have an interview.
It could be a new beginning.'
Pause.
What was her name?

MAN FIVE Margaret.

MAN ONE Poor Margaret.
Silence.
MAN SIX *speaks quietly.*

MAN SIX Same thing happened
to a pal of mine.

MAN ONE Really?

MAN SIX Put me in mind of him.
Hearing you talking.
Jack.
Jack MacKintosh.
Lived round Dagenham somewhere.
He shakes his head.
A tragedy.
He remembers.
Wife died suddenly.
Electrocuted in the bath.
Could have happened to anyone.
It happened to her. To Helen.

Just like that.
Went for a bath.
Said, 'Won't be long Jack.'
He was watching television.
'Just going for a bath.'
And off she went.
Leaving Jack watching television.
Pause.
Up the stairs.
Pause.
Into the bathroom.
Pause.
Running the water.
Pause.
Getting undressed.
Pause.
Climbing in.
Pause.
Reaching out.
Pause.
Switching off the electric fire.
Pause.
Jack was watching television.
Sitting in the lounge, in the dark,
when suddenly . . .
He told me afterwards . . .
Two men were discussing asparagus plants,
when suddenly . . . The screen . . . Went white.
Pause.
Flashed.
Pause.
'Dammit,' he thought, 'the tube's gone.'
Got up.
Turned it off.

Tried to turn the light on.
It wouldn't work.
Stood there.
Stood there in the dark.
Wondering what to do.
Then suddenly remembered Helen.
And went upstairs.
Calling her.
'Helen? You all right love?'
Pause.
Helen not answering.
Jack calling again.
'Helen? You O.K.? It's me. Jack.'
Pause.
Helen not answering.
Pause.
Jack on the landing.
Pause.
In the dark.
Pause.
Groping along.
Pause.
Coming to the bathroom door.
Pause.
Pushing it open.
Pause.
Moving slowly into the steam.
Pause.
'Helen?'
Pause.
Helen not answering.
Pause.
Jack striking a match.
Pause.

Moving to the bath.
Pause.
Looking in.
Silence.
MAN ONE *moves to the ashtray.*

MAN ONE They say
it's a peaceful way to go.

MAN SIX Gas is better.

MAN ONE At two and threepence a Therm!

MAN SIX *laughs, continues reading.*
U.R. door opens suddenly.
MAN THREE *enters.*
*He pauses thoughtfully, closes the door, then moves
slowly to the centre of the room.*
Silence.
He speaks loudly.

MAN THREE Stoke-on-Trent!
The men look at him.
That's a nice town.
He smiles.
That's a very nice town.
MAN SIX *laughs.*
The men look at him.
He lowers the newspaper.

MAN SIX The advert.
Pause.
The Librarian.
Pause.
Fluent Serbian.
He smiles.
Some hopes.
MAN THREE *smiles, and turns to* MAN ONE.

MAN THREE Do you speak it?

MAN ONE Fluently.

MAN THREE *smiles, looks at* MAN FIVE.

  MAN FIVE *looks up.*

MAN THREE Do you?

  MAN FIVE Serbian?

MAN THREE Yes.

  MAN FIVE No.

MAN THREE I was going to say,
           if you did,
           there's an awfully good job
           just waiting for you in Aldershot.
           MAN SIX *smiles.*
           MAN THREE *smiles.*
           MAN FIVE *smiles.*

  MAN ONE But you have other languages.
           A linguistic facility.

  MAN FIVE I studied German for a while.

  MAN ONE Did you?

  MAN FIVE Yes.

           MAN ONE *studies* MAN FIVE *quietly for a moment, then
           speaks sharply.*

  MAN ONE Auto!
           Fahren Sie mich zum Bahnhof!
           MAN THREE *comes to attention.*

MAN THREE Welcher Bahnhof, mein Herr?
           MAN FIVE *looks at them silently.*
           They repeat the routine.

  MAN ONE Auto!
           Fahren Sie mich zum Bahnhof!

MAN THREE Welcher Bahnhof, mein Herr?

  MAN ONE You understand that?

  MAN FIVE I went to evening classes.

MAN THREE How long for?

  MAN FIVE Part of a term.

  MAN ONE But you understood us.

MAN FIVE I only went for a little while.
I couldn't keep it up.
There was the accident.
I began just before . . .
Before she . . .
Pause.
I didn't continue.
MAN THREE He said . . .
MAN ONE I'll tell him.
MAN THREE *makes inviting gesture.*
MAN ONE This is what I said.
I said:
'Taxi!
I want to go to the station!'
And he said . . .
MAN THREE I said:
'Which station, sir?'
Silence.
They repeat the routine.
MAN ONE Auto!
Fahren Sie mich zum Bahnhof!
MAN THREE Welcher Bahnhof, mein Herr?
MAN ONE Say it.
MAN FIVE I'm not sure I could.
MAN ONE Try it.
It's easy.
Come on. Try.
Auto . . .
MAN FIVE *says nothing.*
MAN ONE Come on.
Auto . . .
MAN FIVE Auto . . .
MAN ONE Good!
He turns.

Who says he can't speak German?

MAN THREE *smiles.*

MAN ONE *turns to* MAN FIVE.

Again.

Auto . . .

MAN FIVE Auto . . .

MAN ONE Good!

Now.

Fahren Sie mich zum Bahnhof.

Fahren Sie . . .

MAN FIVE Fahren Sie . . .

MAN ONE Mich . . .

MAN FIVE Mich . . .

MAN ONE *waits.*

MAN FIVE Zum Bahnhof?

MAN ONE Mich zum Bahnhof!

Good! Good!

He turns.

Hey!

Listen to this!

MAN FIVE *smiles.*

MAN ONE Go on. Show them.

Speak German.

MAN FIVE Auto!

MAN ONE Good . . .

MAN FIVE Fahren Sie mich zum Bahnhof!

MAN ONE How about that!

MAN THREE Hooray.

MAN ONE Now the other bit.

MAN FIVE I . . .

MAN ONE Come on.

You're doing marvellously.

Now.

Welcher Bahnhof, mein Herr?

123

Welcher . . .

MAN FIVE Welcher . . .

MAN ONE Welcher Bahnhof, mein Herr ?

Welcher Bahnhof . . .

MAN FIVE Welcher Bahnhof . . .

MAN ONE Yes ?

MAN FIVE Mein Herr ?

MAN ONE Good! Good!

Now.

Pause.

He shouts very loudly.

Auto!

Fahren Sie mich zum Bahnhof!

MAN FIVE Welcher Bahnhof, mein Herr ?

MAN ONE Again!

MAN FIVE Welcher Bahnhof, mein Herr ?

MAN ONE Again!

MAN FIVE Welcher Bahnhof, mein Herr ?

He laughs.

MAN ONE Again!

MAN FIVE Welcher Bahnhof . . . Mein Herr ?

MAN ONE Again!

MAN FIVE Welcher Bahnhof . . . Mein Herr ?

He laughs.

MAN ONE Again!

Say it again!

Speak German!

Speak German!

MAN FIVE Welcher . . .

He laughs.

Welcher Bahnhof . . .

He laughs.

Mein Herr ?

Welcher Bahnhof . . . Mein Herr ?

Welcher Bahnhof . . . Mein Herr ?
He continues laughing, and repeating the German phrase.
The men turn away.
He sees them, and stops, confused.
U.L. door opens suddenly.
He turns, frightened.
The men look up.
SECRETARY *enters.*
She smiles pleasantly.

SECRETARY Mr [*Full name of* MAN ONE].

MAN ONE *goes to the chairs, collects his things, moves towards the U.L. door.*
He stops, and returns to MAN SIX.
MAN SIX *hands him the newspaper.*
MAN ONE *moves towards the U.L. door.*
He pauses in front of MAN FIVE.
MAN FIVE *looks back silently.*
MAN ONE *smiles, and goes through the U.L. door.*
SECRETARY *follows.*
The door closes.
Silence.
MAN SIX *moves to a chair, and sits.*
MAN THREE *stands quietly.*
MAN FIVE *looks at his wristwatch, the room so dark now he has to tilt it towards the source of light where, in silhouette,* MAN TWO *is standing.*
The men wait.
Long pause.
MAN FIVE *rises, and moves to the U.R. door.*
He opens it, and goes out.
The door closes.
Blackout.

2 WASHROOM

*Light flashes on behind back panel of Waiting Room,
revealing box-like Washroom lined with mirrors.*
Silence.
The door opens.
MAN FIVE *enters.*
He can be seen with infinite clarity, but cannot be heard.
He looks round the Washroom, then closes the door.
*He removes his jacket, hangs it behind the door, crosses
to a washbasin, and fills it with water.*
*He rolls up his sleeves, puts his hands in the water, and
raises them to his face.*
*He holds them to his face, then lowers them, and looks at
his face in a mirror.*
He touches his face.
Pause.
He reaches for a towel, and dabs his face dry.
He puts down the towel, and brings out a comb.
He combs his hair carefully, and puts the comb away.
He turns his head, and listens.
Pause.
*He rolls down his sleeves, crosses to the door, takes down
his jacket, and puts it on.*
*He looks at himself in a mirror, and adjusts his tie, and
his hair.*
*He straightens his jacket, turns, looks round the Wash-
room, and listens.*
Pause.
He opens the door, and goes out.
The door closes.
Blackout.

3 WAITING ROOM

A dark silence.
U.R. door opens suddenly.
MAN FIVE *enters, looks round the room, then closes the door.*
He crosses to his chair, and sits.
Pause.
U.L. door opens suddenly.
A shaft of light spills into the room, illuminating the empty chairs.
The men look up.
SECRETARY *enters.*
She smiles pleasantly.

SECRETARY Mr [*Full name of* MAN THREE].

MAN THREE *comes out of the darkness, and goes through the U.L. door.*

SECRETARY *crosses the room, and raises her hand to a switch.*

A blinding light comes on, throwing the room into garish relief.

MAN TWO *stands quietly.*

MAN SIX *has gone.*

SECRETARY *lowers her hand, re-crosses the room, smiles at* MAN FIVE, *and goes through the U.L. door.*

The door closes.

Silence.

MAN TWO *turns slowly to* MAN FIVE.

MAN FIVE *looks back silently.*

MAN TWO *moves to the centre of the room.*

He smiles.

MAN TWO When were you there?

Pause.

Newton Abbot.

MAN FIVE Oh.

He smiles

I forget when exactly.

MAN TWO Before or after?

Pause.

The boating accident.

Pause.

MAN FIVE After.

Pause.

MAN TWO She wasn't with you then.

Pause.

Margaret.

Pause.

MAN FIVE No.

MAN TWO *moves nearer to* MAN FIVE.

MAN TWO You only passed through, you say.

Pause.

MAN FIVE Yes.

Pause.

MAN TWO Where were you going again?

Pause.

MAN FIVE Barnstaple.

Pause.

MAN TWO Why?

Pause.

MAN FIVE I had to see someone there.

Pause.

MAN TWO Who?

Pause.

MAN FIVE A friend.

Pause.

MAN TWO To do with the accident?

Pause.

MAN FIVE Yes.

Pause.

MAN TWO I see.

Pause.

And all this happened nine months ago.

Pause.

MAN FIVE Eight.

Pause.

MAN TWO Where?

Pause.

MAN FIVE Salcombe.

Pause.

MAN TWO Did you stay long in Barnstaple?

Pause.

MAN FIVE A week.

Pause.

MAN TWO You travelled by car?

Pause.

MAN FIVE Yes.

Pause.

MAN TWO All the way?

Pause.

MAN FIVE Yes.

Pause.

MAN TWO All the way by car. From Salcombe to Barnstaple.

Pause.

MAN FIVE Yes.

Pause.

MAN TWO Via Newton Abbot.

Pause.

MAN FIVE Yes.

They face each other silently.

MAN TWO May I see a photograph?

Pause.

Of Margaret.

Pause.

Do you have one?

MAN FIVE *takes a photograph from a wallet.*

He rises, and crosses to MAN TWO.

He hands him the photograph.

MAN TWO *studies it silently, and hands it back.*

Thank you.

MAN FIVE *puts it away.*

MAN TWO *faces front.*

I've never been down that way myself.

Pause.

Dorset's my stamping ground.

Pause.

I expect you've been there.

Pause.

Have you?

Pause.

MAN FIVE No.

Pause.

MAN TWO Are you going?

Pause.

Don't you know?

Pause.

MAN FIVE I may. One day.

Pause.

MAN TWO Not planning to, right?

Pause.

In the near future I mean.

He turns to MAN FIVE.

They face each other without moving.

U.L. door opens suddenly.
MAN FIVE *turns.*
SECRETARY *enters.*
She smiles pleasantly.
SECRETARY Mr [*Full name of* MAN FIVE].
 MAN FIVE *pauses, then turns to* MAN TWO.
 This way please.
 MAN FIVE *pauses, moves to a chair, and collects his things.*
 He looks back at MAN TWO, *then at* SECRETARY.
 Both stand silently.
 MAN FIVE *moves to the U.L. door.*
 He reaches it, looks through it, and stops.
 Long silence.
 He backs slowly to the centre of the room.
 Long silence.
 MAN ONE *comes through the U.L. door.*
 He stops, and looks at MAN FIVE.
 MAN THREE *comes through the U.L. door.*
 He stops, and looks at MAN FIVE.
 MAN FOUR *comes through the U.L. door.*
 He stops, and looks at MAN FIVE.
 MAN SIX *comes through the U.L. door.*
 He stops, and looks at MAN FIVE.
 MAN SEVEN *comes through the U.L. door.*
 He stops, and looks at MAN FIVE.
 MAN EIGHT *comes through the U.L. door, reading a file.*
 He stops, and looks at MAN FIVE.
 SECRETARY *closes the U.L. door.*
 She turns, and looks at MAN FIVE.
 MAN FIVE *looks round at the men.*
 They look back at him silently.
 The lights fade slowly.
 Curtain.

131

INVASION
A SCENARIO

Invasion was first produced by BBC Television on 10 April 1969. THE HOSTESS was played by Libby Morris, THE HOST by Tony Bilbow, their GUESTS by Michael Coles, Polly Elwes, and Denys Hawthorne. The play was directed by Donald McWhinnie in collaboration with the author.

A dinner party.

The Host and Hostess are entertaining three guests (one woman and two men).

Their conversation (unscripted) is friendly and informal.

In a dark adjoining room (divided from the dining room by a half-open louvred partition), scenes of horror are flickering across a television screen.

They have the broken grainy quality of documentary film.

They show the Americans at war in Vietnam.

The scenes, which are in black and white, follow no particular sequence.

They form a non-stop montage (without commentary) which has the atmosphere of a dream.

At certain fixed points (see below), specially constructed scenes of unprecedented horror and suffering are shown in close-up.

It is at these points that the people at dinner (with the exception of The Hostess) become aware of the pictures on the screen and involved in the action and the crossfire.

One by one they die.

The dining room, at the hands of unseen forces, itself becomes a scene of massacre and death, united at last with the horrors that invaded it from the screen.

Abbreviations: (TVS) = Television Screen (Black and White)
                 (DP)   = Dinner Party (Colour)

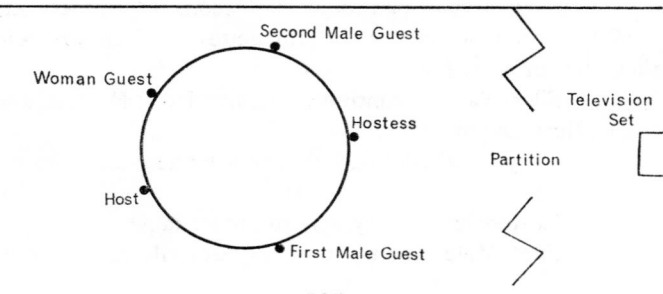

Sequence 1

OPENING

(TVS) Pilot in aircraft. Silence.

Blackout. Caption. INVASION.

(TVS) Pilot continued.

Blackout. Caption. BY BARRY BERMANGE.

(TVS) Long shot of aircraft banking then diving and firing rockets.

Ground. The rockets bursting. A village being destroyed.

Intercut with

(DP) Flash shots of Host, Hostess, guests, smiling, smoking, drinking martinis.

(TVS) Close-ups of devastation following the air attack. Silence.

Intercut with

(DP) Group shots of party people smiling.

(TVS) Close-ups continued. Spasmodic laughter of guests over.

Slow circular pan round dark room. Light flickering from television screen on to silhouettes of furniture and glittering surfaces. Laughter over.

Silence as pan continues to frame Host, Hostess, and guests, through partition.

They stand talking, but cannot be heard.

Hold.

Hostess leads everybody to dinner table.

First Male Guest pauses momentarily as he passes

the half-open partition, gazes into the dark room at the screen, then continues to the table.

Host lights candles, pours wine.

They commence eating the already served *hors d'oeuvre.*

Hold, framing the diners through the partition.

Then cut to the table.

Conversation [*ad libitum*] up to Sequence 2.

Sequence 2

DEATH OF THE FIRST MALE GUEST

(DP) Conversation [*ad libitum*] continuing. Close-ups of eaters, drinkers, talkers.

Intercut with

(TVS) Flash shots of film.

They become more insistent.

(DP) The attention of the First Male Guest is drawn slowly to the screen.

(TVS) Horror Sequence (A) begins.

(DP) The First Male Guest watches impassively.

The party conversation continues around him.

(TVS) The horror sequence develops.

A rhythmic cutting sequence begins between the horrors on the screen and the face of the First Male Guest.

Intercut with

(DP) Flash shots of the party people smiling.

Horror Sound begins.

(DP) Slow panning shot of the party people eating, drinking, talking, as though behind a sheet of glass. Horror Sound over.

Increase Horror Sound as pan continues.

The First Male Guest comes into camera.

Move in to big close-up.

The colour drains slowly from his face as physically he becomes involved in the action of the horror film.

Rhythmic cutting sequence develops.

Peak Horror Sound.

Cut to silence.

(TVS) Final shots of horror sequence with face of the First Male Guest (now black and white) included.

The sequence ends.

(DP) Panning shot round table. Silence.

Host pouring drinks.

Woman Guest and Second Male Guest smiling pleasantly as Hostess serves the first course.

Pan continues to discover First Male Guest sprawled across the table. He is dead and covered in blood.

Cutaway shots of chair tipped over on to its side, ruckled carpet, broken china vase.

The body of the First Male Guest is ignored by the others.

Conversation [*ad libitum*] up to sequence 3.

Sequence 3

DEATH OF WOMAN GUEST AND HOST

(DP) Conversation [*ad libitum*] continuing. Close-ups of eaters, drinkers, talkers.

Intercut with body of the First Male Guest, and (TVS) Flash shots of film.

They become more insistent.

(DP) The attention first of the Woman Guest then the Host is drawn slowly to the screen.

(TVS) Horror Sequence (B) begins.

(DP) The Woman Guest and Host watch impassively.

The party conversation continues around them, i.e. a dualogue between the Second Male Guest and Hostess.

(TVS) The horror sequence develops.

A rhythmic cutting sequence begins between the horrors on the screen and the faces of the Woman Guest and Host.

Intercut with

(DP) Flash shots of Second Male Guest and Hostess, and flash shots of body of the First Male Guest.

Horror Sound begins.

(DP) Panning shot of the Second Male Guest and Hostess eating, drinking, talking, as though behind a sheet of glass. Horror Sound over.

Increase Horror Sound as pan continues.

The Woman Guest and Host come into camera.

Move in to big close-ups.

The colour drains slowly from their faces as physically they become involved in the action of the horror film.

Rhythmic cutting sequence develops.

Peak Horror Sound.

Cut to silence.

(TVS) Final shots of horror sequence with faces of Woman Guest and Host (now black and white) included.

The sequence ends.

(DP) Panning shot round table. Silence.

Second Male Guest pouring drinks.

Hostess smiling pleasantly.

Pan continues to discover the Woman Guest and Host lying twisted on the floor, both dead and covered in blood.

Cutaway shots of torn and blackened wallpaper, broken china, glass, and windows, knocked over lamps, a door hanging off its hinges.

The bodies of the Woman Guest, Host, and First Male Guest are ignored by the others.

Conversation [*ad libitum*) up to Sequence 4.

Sequence 4

DEATH OF SECOND MALE GUEST

(DP) Conversation [*ad libitum*] continuing. Close-ups of Second Male Guest and Hostess eating, drinking, talking.

Intercut with bodies of Woman Guest, Host, and First Male Guest, and

(TVS) Flash shots of film.

They become more insistent.

(DP) The attention of the Second Male Guest is drawn slowly to the screen.

(TVS) Horror Sequence (C) begins.

(DP) The Second Male Guest watches impassively.

The Hostess continues talking.

(TVS) The horror sequence develops.

A rhythmic cutting sequence begins between the horrors on the screen and the face of the Second Male Guest.

Intercut with

(DP) Flash shots of Hostess, and flash shots of bodies of Woman Guest, Host, and First Male Guest.

Horror Sound begins.

(DP) Shot of Hostess eating, drinking, talking, as though behind a sheet of glass. Horror Sound over.

Increase Horror Sound as camera crabs to Second

Male Guest.

Move in to big close-up.

The colour drains slowly from his face as physically he becomes involved in the action of the horror film.

Rhythmic cutting sequence develops.

Peak Horror Sound.

Cut to silence.

(TVS) Final shots of horror sequence with face of Second Male Guest (now black and white) included.

The sequence ends with a series of still photographs showing the burned and mutilated bodies of men, women, and children.

These link directly with

(DP) (now black and white).

Shot of Second Male Guest lying dead at the foot of a machine-gunned wall.

Shot of body of Woman Guest on floor.

Shot of body of Host on floor.

Shot of body of First Male Guest across table.

Pan slowly round devastated room, parts of which are burning.

Fade up sound of crying child.

Pan slowly back to dinner table as colour returns to the room, for Sequence 5.

Sequence 5

CLOSING

The Hostess eating her dessert.
The child crying.
Move in, framing Hostess.

Move slowly past Hostess towards half-open louvred partition.

Blackout.
Silence.
Captions.

Methuen's Modern Plays

Edited by John Cullen

Shelagh Delaney	A TASTE OF HONEY
	THE LION IN LOVE
Max Frisch	THE FIRE RAISERS
	ANDORRA
Jean Giraudoux	TIGER AT THE GATES
	DUEL OF ANGELS
Rolf Hochhuth	THE REPRESENTATIVE
Heinar Kipphardt	IN THE MATTER OF J. ROBERT OPPENHEIMER
Arthur Kopit	CHAMBER MUSIC and other plays
Jakov Lind	THE SILVER FOXES ARE DEAD and other plays
Henry Livings	KELLY'S EYE and other plays
	EH?
John Mortimer	TWO STARS FOR COMFORT
	THE JUDGE
Joe Orton	CRIMES OF PASSION
	LOOT
	WHAT THE BUTLER SAW
Harold Pinter	THE BIRTHDAY PARTY
	THE ROOM and THE DUMB WAITER
	THE CARETAKER
	A SLIGHT ACHE and other plays
	THE COLLECTION and THE LOVER
	THE HOMECOMING
	TEA PARTY and other plays
	LANDSCAPE and SILENCE
Jean-Paul Sartre	CRIME PASSIONNEL
Theatre Workshop and Charles Chilton	OH WHAT A LOVELY WAR